The Story of the TRAIN

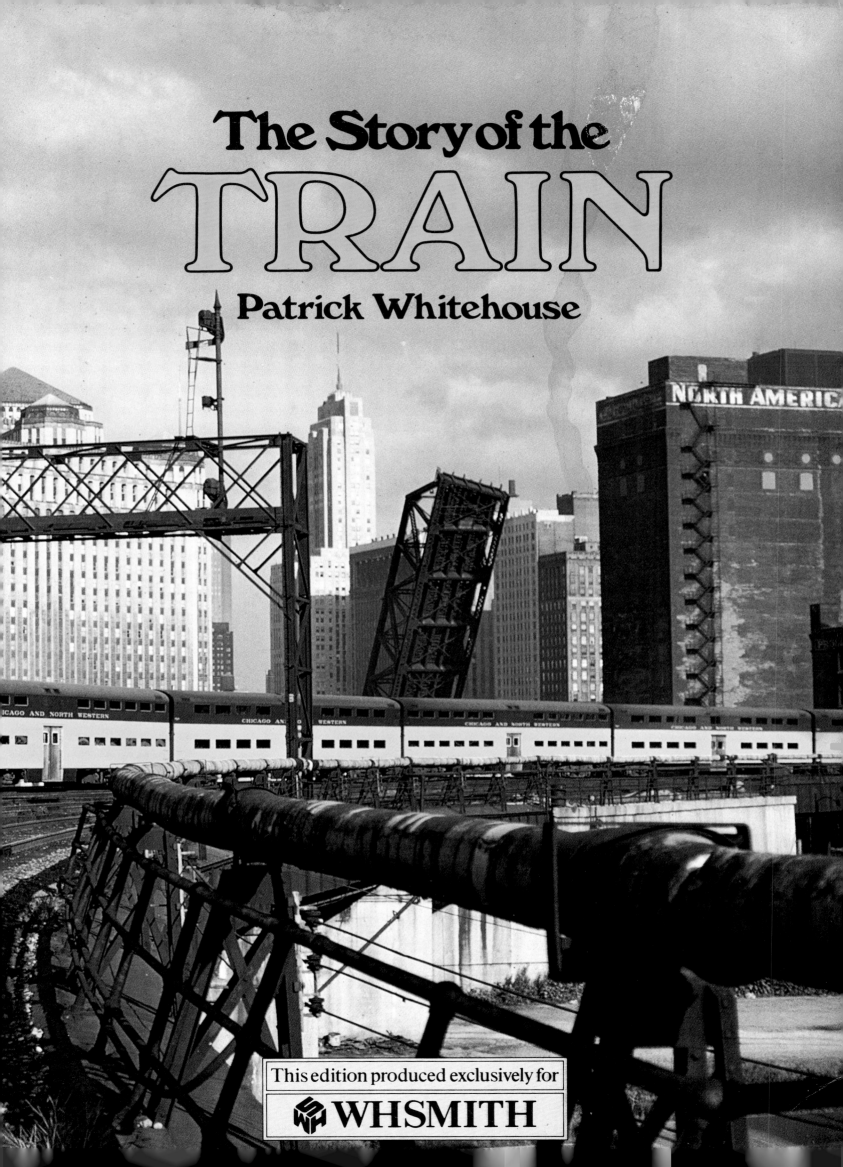

The Story of the
TRAIN

Patrick Whitehouse

Author's acknowledgments

No book of this nature can be written without recourse to vital works of reference and I would like to make it clear that these have been used. Many of the books which I have consulted have been written by authors who are personal friends and I would like to thank them for their readable and valuable contents. They include *The Illustrated History of Railways in Britain* (Marshall Cavendish 1979), *Railways, Past, Present and Future* (Orbis 1982) and *Luxury Trains* (Bison Books 1979) by Geoffrey Freeman Allen together with *Steam Passenger Locomotives* by J.B. Hollingsworth (Salamander Books 1982). I have also consulted *History of Railways* (New English Library 1974), *Railway Magazine, The Locomotive Magazine, Railway Wonders of the World* and the China Railway Publishing House, whom I especially wish to thank for their co-operation and assistance.

I should also like to thank the Editor of *Railway Magazine*, John Slater, for permission to use material contained therein. To those photographers who have travelled the world to obtain excellent transparencies, including Peter Howard, Jim Jarvis and John Snell, I record my thanks and admiration.

Photographic acknowledgments

John Adams: 9, 10, 41 bottom; John Alosa: 106 bottom; P.M. Alexander: 39, 41 top; British Columbia Railways: 56; Canadian National Railways: 14, 57, 81 top; Crown Copyright National Railway Museum: 23; D.B.: 70, 81 bottom; P. Harris: 22, 54; P.J. Howard: 64, 66, 67, 68–69, 74 top, 76, 81, 97, 116; Japanese Tourist Office: 91, 92 top; J.M. Jarvis: 39, 117; K.P. Lawrence: 40, 59; Millbrook House: 6, 7, 9, 11, 12, 15, 21 left, 23, 26, 28, 42, 43, 44, 45 bottom, 50, 51 top, 128; Novosti Press Agency: 82, 83; O.B.B.: 77; W.A. Pearce: 46, 108; Courtesy Railway Magazine: 11, 29, 30, 32, 33, 34, 51 bottom; Railway & Travel Monthly: 24; Mrs D.A. Robinson: 78–79; S.A.R.: 101; S.B.B.: 72–73; S.N.C.F.: 71, 74 bottom; J.B. Snell: 48–49, 60; Swiss National Tourist Office: 126–127; Eric Treacy: 28, 53, 55, 65: Venice Simplon Orient Express Photographic Library: 18; The Government of Western Australia: 104, 106 top; C.N. Whitehouse: 94; P.B. Whitehouse Collection: title spread, 8, 12, 13, 16, 17, 19, 20, 21 top, 22, 27, 28, 31, 33, 35, 36, 37, 38, 45 top, 47, 58, 60, 62–63, 85, 86–87, 88, 92 bottom, 93, 95, 97, 100, 102, 103, 110, 111, 114, 115, 118, 119, 120, 121, 123, 124; Bruce Worthington: 107.

Front cover: A BR Western Region express leaving the Severn tunnel in 1961 (P.B. Whitehouse Collection)

Back cover: QJ 2-10-2 with train about to pass under the Great Wall of China (P.B. Whitehouse Collection)

**This edition produced exclusively for
W H Smith**

Published by
Deans International Publishing
52–54 Southwark Street, London SE1 1UA
A division of The Hamlyn Publishing Group Limited
London · New York · Sydney · Toronto

Copyright © The Hamlyn Publishing Group Limited 1984
ISBN 0 603 03594 9

Printed and bound by Graficromo s.a., Cordoba, Spain

Contents

19th Century Railways   6

Early Train Travel   19

Famous Express Trains   29

When Steam Was King   40

Trains in the West   64

Trains in the East   82

Trains in Africa and Australasia   95

Railways of Character   110

19th-Century Railways

The north-east of England was the cradle of Britain's railways long before the use of steam.
Colliery tubs and wagons ran over plateways where flanged wrought-iron rails contained the wheels of the vehicles. This scene of 1773 at Newcastle colliery shows the normal method of operation. The full tub would roll down to the canal or waterway by gravity and return horsedrawn.

Contrary to popular thinking, George Stephenson did not invent the steam locomotive, neither did he produce the first engine to run on rails. The latter achievement was the 'brainchild' of a Cornish pumping machinery engineer, Richard Trevithick, who had demonstrated a steam carriage in London during the first years of the century. Trevithick was retained by Samuel Homfray, the owner of the Pen-y-Darren iron works in South Wales, where he adapted a stationary steam engine for use on the works track which was, in fact, a plateway. This event occurred on 13 February 1804 and the crude machine won Homfray a wager of 500 guineas.

By that date railways had been in use, mainly in mining areas, for nearly 50 years. Indeed horsedrawn carts had been pulled along angled iron plates at Coalbrookdale in Shropshire in 1767. Unfortunately for Trevithick (and any immediate recognition and progress), the iron plates shattered under the locomotive's weight and it returned to its originally intended duties as a stationary engine. The technical problem of supporting the weight of the locomotive had yet to be solved.

As industry grew, the problem of the movement of goods around the Western world had been solved in the main by the building of canals. In Britain, for instance, the construction of artificial waterways goes back to the mid-1500s when the Exeter Canal was built. But it

Richard Trevithick's demonstration in Euston Square as early as 1809 – colloquially known as Catch as Catch Can. From a Science Museum print.

was the mid-1700s which saw the commercial success of canal building. However, canals were only at their best where the countryside was flat, and in many cases mineral wealth was being dug from mines and quarries in hilly areas which could connect with no waterway system. For many years a primitive form of wooden rail was used underground. After the Coalbrookdale experiment it was soon found that an iron wheel on an iron rail gave free running which, in turn, allowed larger horsedrawn loads to be carried. It did not take long for it to be realized that a flanged wheel running on the surface of a metal rail was even better; the problem now was that the short fish-bellied iron rails were still not strong enough for any great weight.

The difficulty was overcome at Wylam Colliery near Newcastle where its superintendent, William Hedley, saw the answer in applying power to more than one pair of locomotive wheels. This was achieved by a cog drive and the work was done in the blacksmith's shop under the foreman, Timothy Hackworth, who was later to become George Stephenson's resident engineer for the Stockton & Darlington Railway. The first engines were *Puffing Billy* and *Wylam Dilly*.

The man who saw the real prospect of development was George Stephenson who was born alongside the route of the Wylam tramway in 1781. A self-taught man whose father had worked in the mines, Stephenson was enginewright for all the collieries based at Killingworth, Northumberland, by the time he was 31. It was less than a year after *Puffing Billy* first stormed past his birthplace at Wylam that Stephenson sought support from his employer, the mine owner Lord Ravensworth, to build his own locomotive; the result was *Blucher*, built in 1814. But the pattern in the kaleidoscope of travel was beginning to take shape. As far back as 1801 Parliament had granted an Act for a line of track which was intended to run from Wandsworth on the river Thames to Croydon, with the hope of reaching Portsmouth. The principle was that this 'railway' would be used like a canal for the use of which privately owned horsedrawn vehicles would pay a toll.

It was left to northern Quaker businessman Edward Pease to obtain Parliament's assent for a further public tramway, this time in the

county of Durham, linking the town of Darlington to the port of Stockton for the conveyance of coal, iron, lime, corn and other commodities. The Act was granted in 1821 and George Stephenson persuaded Edward Pease to appoint him the line's engineer at a salary of £300 per year. The stage was set for the railways of the world.

Naturally Stephenson made strong representations for steam traction, and in spite of severe misgivings by the Stockton & Darlington Railway directors this was adopted for most of the line's length. The railway was opened with considerable ceremony on 27 September 1825 with Stephenson's *Locomotion* running the 21 miles from Shildon to Stockton with a load of 69 tons including accommodation for the directors and wagons fitted with wooden benches. It was not long before the industrial world was agog, for not only was the line efficient, it was, by force of this efficiency, profitable: dividends were as high as 14 per cent (a huge amount in those days) by the early 1830s. It was a trip to England to see the line which resulted in another Quaker, Evan Thomas, returning to the U.S.A. (at Baltimore) to persuade his businessmen colleagues to change their plans from the building of a canal to the construction of a railway. Thus was born the Baltimore & Ohio Railroad which opened on 24 April 1827. France followed suit with a line out of the St. Etienne coal field on 1 October 1828, and the Austrians had started the year before.

Progress was not slow in North America. Colonel John Stevens, a thoughtful New Jersey farmer, had been considering the use of steam

Right: The early railways, including the Stockton & Darlington of 1825, used stone sets, not wooden sleepers, for the bases to their rails. These with wrought-iron rails made a firm but very rigid track.

Below: Freight is the mainstay of railways throughout the world and has been from the very beginning. This print of freight trains on the Liverpool & Manchester Railway shows not only the carriage of goods and livestock (with attendants) but also the more stable inside-cylindered locomotives which followed the earlier Rocket design.

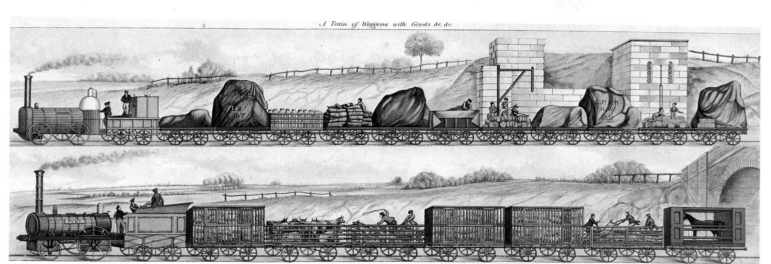

A Train of Waggons with Goods &c. &c.

power, even to the point of producing his own boiler, and by 1812 he was satisfied in his own mind that railways, not canals, were the transport of the future. Like Trevithick he had little early support and his steam engine ran round on a circle of track on his own property at Hoboken in 1825. But other thinking Americans were recognizing the potential of railways as well.

The great American West was still virtually unexplored at this time and although the eastern seaboard was well served with waterways, including the new Erie Canal linking Buffalo to the Atlantic, there were anxious thoughts as to how to progress westwards beyond the Allegheny Mountains. It was a canal company, the Delaware & Hudson, which eventually decided to extend its waterway for the last 16 miles of the proposed route by a railway, part rope-worked over inclined planes and part locomotive-hauled. The firm sent a youthful engineer, Horatio Allen, to England to buy locomotives, four of which, *America, Hudson, Delaware* and *Stourbridge Lion,* arrived in New York in 1829. Other lines followed suit and by 1830 the Baltimore & Ohio was announcing cash prizes of $4,000 and $3,500 for the most proficient four-wheeled locomotives, built to the company's specification. A start had been made in securing a firm foothold for the railways of North America. President Andrew Jackson made the very first Presidential railway journey on the Baltimore & Ohio.

It was Britain's Liverpool & Manchester Railway which transformed the whole concept of rail transportation. Built by Stephenson, this was the world's first passenger railway and the first-ever design for intercity linking. Double tracked from the beginning, and with considerable engineering works including the 70-ft (21-m) deep Olive Mount cutting hewn out of stone and the crossing of Chat Moss bog, this successful investment took the country and the world into a railway-building boom. It was shortly followed by the Grand Junction south from Manchester, and the capital's first main line, the London & Birmingham. From this time onwards tracks were to spread like spider webs as railway fever intensified. It was the period of the railway Barons, of the evolution of the engineers, and of the beginning of the great contractors: Hudson, George and Robert Stephenson, Brunel and Brassy were but a few. This, too, was the time of the huge

The first main line railway to serve the capital was the London & Birmingham of 1838. Both termini were served by monumental buildings symbolizing the railway's ambition and its standing in the brave new world of transport. That at Curzon Street, Birmingham still stands, though the train sheds themselves have been destroyed to form a freight complex.

roving force of vagabond labour called the 'navvies', a name drawn from the canal-building days of 'inland navigators'. Paid at piecework rates and living rough, it is said that they could shift some 20 cubic yards (over 20 tons) of spoil per head, per day. By this means, and this means alone, the railway network grew; cuttings were excavated; embankments were built; viaducts and tunnels were completed in brick and stone. For 40 years some 50,000 navvies were employed continuously. In the peak year, 1847, over a quarter of a million were at work in Britain alone.

Fortunately, the railways constructed immediately after the Stockton & Darlington were built to the same gauge – 4 ft $8\frac{1}{2}$ in. This rather odd distance between the rails was determined by the width of the wagonways in the northeast of England. This track width was probably in its turn set by the widest truck able to be pushed by a colliery worker on his own. With the Stephenson family closely allied to the new line it was natural that other trunk railways would follow the established norm. But there was one man who thought otherwise: his name was Isambard Kingdom Brunel.

Son of an immigrant engineer, Marc Brunel, whose work on the Thames tunnel was held in high repute, the young Brunel made his name as the designer of the Clifton Suspension Bridge over the Avon

An early print showing a London & Birmingham Railway train near Camden. Note the Rocket-type locomotive with its cylinders at the firebox end.

One of the Great Western Railway's 7 ft 0¼ in gauge trains headed by a Gooch 4-2-2. The extra width allowed by this Broad Gauge ensured not only roomy coaching stock but also much smoother riding.

Gorge at Bristol. He applied for and obtained the post of chief engineer to the embryonic Great Western Railway, a line to join Bristol with London, and a railway to leave its mark for ever on the transport map of the world.

Brunel was a man of great imagination and considerable engineering skill. His aim was to join the two cities with a line of easy gradients and daring designs; this was done by careful surveying and the contribution of superb pieces of civil engineering such as the flat arched viaduct at Maidenhead and the famous Box tunnel near Bath, but the line purposely avoided nearly every large town en route. To the horror of other railways but to his director's satisfaction, Brunel chose a gauge of 7 ft 0¼ in.

The 'Broad Gauge', as it was called, certainly had considerable advantages. Its width allowed for extra comfort in its coaches and stability in its stock; it also made higher speeds not only possible but readily achievable. The snag was that the Great Western and its connections, the Bristol, Exeter & South Devon Railways were alone in the field; when junctions were made with other lines the problems of traffic interchange were costly and time-consuming. Eventually a Parliamentary Commission decided that no further Broad Gauge lines could be constructed and by 1892 the whole Great Western system was converted to the standard 4 ft 8½ in gauge. For many years mixed-gauge tracks were in use, allowing trains of both gauges to run over the sections concerned.

Meanwhile tracks spread their net over most of Europe, though here State control took preference over the private enterprise of Britain and North America. The German states followed the French and Austrians and at the opening of the Berlin-Potsdam line the Crown Prince (who was later to become King Friedrich Wilhelm IV of Prussia) is said to have proclaimed that 'no human arm will ever stop the progress of this car which will roll throughout the world'. The strategic and logistical significance of the railway was not lost on the German mind from its inception.

Below: This print from the Illustrated London News, *shows the chaos resulting from the trans-shipment of goods where the two gauges (Great Western and Midland Railways) met at Gloucester.*

Right: The Czar laid the foundation stone for the Trans-Siberian Railway (then named the International Railway) in 1891 and the line was virtually complete ten years later, though passengers had to cross Lake Baikal by a British-built train ferry. This early postcard of a Russian train around the turn of the century is typical of the period. Note the wide 5 ft 0 in gauge track.

Russia also saw the significance of the railway and the Czar ordered a feasibility study of a St. Petersburg to Moscow line in 1841; he even sent engineers to investigate American railway practice, trying to compare like with like in the wide open spaces. The result of the American visit was a foregone conclusion and in 1843 the railway was started. It took ten years to build, using a vast horde of 50,000 serfs for the 406-mile route. The Russians decided on a gauge of 5 ft 0 in on the advice of an American, George Washington Whistler; Russian railway experts had put forward a gauge of 6 ft 0 in.

By 1875, just 50 years after the opening of the Stockton & Darlington, the railway was the principal transport system all over Europe. The reasons for its development were political, economic (the

chemin de fer

Africa's first railway system was born in Egypt, dating from 1852 with its main line running from Cairo to Aswan. This print shows a scene at the southern terminus close to the river Nile in the early part of this century.

growth of industrialization), and, to a large degree, military. Not all mainland European railways were state-owned originally but it was generally not long before the various governments intervened: control was seen to be of vital national importance, though the French evaded this issue until the late 1930s.

The patterns set, progress could not be withstood. In Europe it was the interlinkage of towns and industry; in North America it was expansion. In fact there is an aphorism which states that in Europe nations built their railways and in North America railways built the nation. Without doubt the U.S.A. and Canada were both transformed by railway transport. By the middle of the century the U.S.A. had over 9,000 miles of railway – far more than that of any other country. In the main the early extension of the American railways can be attributed to the financial spur of the American system of awarding government land grants. By the beginning of the Civil War in 1861, the country had built over 30,000 miles of railway. On 10 May 1869 the Union Pacific Railroad met the Central Pacific at Promentory Point, Utah, thereby completing the first great transcontinental route. The event was celebrated by the driving in of a golden spike. But this was only the beginning; by the 1890s four more such lines were completed mainly by those working for the great tycoons like Commodore Vanderbilt (to whom was attributed the phrase 'law, what do I care about law? Haven't I got the power?'), Daniel Drew and Jay Gould.

This print, from a painting by A. Sherriff Scott R.C.A., shows the Montreal & Lachine Railroad being opened in 1847. The Hon. James Ferrier, founder and president of the railway, is inviting Lord Elgin to inaugurate the service.

In Canada growth was much slower. In spite of an early start in 1836, the first trunk route was not completed until 1885, but from then on the country's mileage tripled to 30,000 miles. In the end, two transcontinental routes evolved: the Canadian Pacific; and the other interconnecting lines which were eventually, in 1917, taken over by the Canadian Government as the Canadian National Railway.

South, beyond the isthmus of Panama, growth was much slower; no progress was made until after the consolidation of the independent states. Had this occurred some 50 years earlier one wonders if South America would have given birth to the railway, as Richard Trevithick was in Peru in 1816 installing pumping engines and making sketches of a nine-mile line from Lima to its port at Callão: this line was eventually built in 1851, closely followed in 1852 by railways in Chile and Brazil. The Lima line, as the Central of Peru, was extended over the Andes to Huancayo, tapping en route the great silver mines

around Oroya. It was British owned, and its summit the highest ever at over 15,000 ft (4,572 m).

Because the South American states have been largely impecunious their railways have been foreign backed (mostly British and American) in the search of beef and minerals; their gauges, particularly in the Andean northwest, have often been narrow as these were cheaper to build and allowed sharper curves and switchbacks. There were other reasons for adopting specific gauges too. For instance, the Buenos Aires Western Railway adopted the 5 ft 6 in gauge because it acquired two locomotives of that gauge originally destined for India (the engines had been put into use during the Crimean War and were then surplus). Chile adopted the same gauge but not on the east side of the Andes section, but did not link it up with the west side because that section, the Trans-Andean Railway, was metre. South American

Left: A print from the Illustrated London News *showing a railborne gun battery built for the American Federal Government in 1861 by Baldwin. It was proposed to carry 50 riflemen and a rifled cannon capable of bearing through the end slot.*

railways had (and have) some of the most spectacular and magnificent lines in the world. Equally spectacular were (and are) the systems of operation with slick working up and down switchbacks on mountain sections and even passenger train attendants equipped with oxygen cylinders to compensate for the rarified air over 10,000 feet up.

As the Victorian era moved into its second half, Western nations had begun to look east and south for trade and consolidation. Colonies sprang up and prospered in Africa, India and Australasia. Railways were needed to assist this development. Of these, India acquired what was probably the most rationally planned railway system in the whole of the 19th century, largely due to one of its great Governor Generals, Lord Dalhousie. The policy was that the British Government would guarantee a dividend of not less than 5 per cent (a high investment rate in those days) with the right to ordain the routes and to take over

Above: The U.S.A. was transformed by its railways. Much of the work was done by immigrant help. This early print of the Central Pacific Railroad shows a train about to enter a snow protection shed cheered on by Chinese workers.

15

the railway if it so wished after 20 years. Railways had to be constructed to laid-down standards and naturally fitted into both military and internal security requirements.

Britain also saw to it that similar strategic lines were constructed in Burma, and the Dutch took a similar view in the East Indies (Java and Sumatra).

Australia was not an inviting proposition for railways; the early settlers put down their roots on the coast and mountains barred the way into the hinterland. But if the country was to be developed then government aid was essential and, as there were few or no navigable rivers, railways were the only viable solutions. Australia's first railway was a horse tramway in South Australia from Gwoola to Port Elliot at the mouth of the Murray River. The first steam line was the 2½-mile long Melbourne & Hobson's Bay Railway from Flinders Street, Melbourne, to Port Melbourne in Victoria. Most lines were built in the south and east and until this century Western Australia had no link whatsoever with the rest of the country.

Like South America, Australia was (and still is) beset by a variety of gauges. The three pioneer states of New South Wales, Victoria, and

Below: The Indian standard gauge of 5 ft 6 in was also adopted for the principal lines in Ceylon (Sri Lanka). One of the most magnificent is that running from the capital Colombo on the coast to Kandy in the central highlands. This scene shows one of the standard 4-6-0s with a train at Sensation Point in 1905.

Two stations around the turn of the century: above right, Dresden – a typical example of a large German station, part terminus, part through platforms. The scene, except for the motor traffic, is very much the same today; right, Marylebone – the last main line terminus to be built in London was the showpiece of the Great Central Railway which did not enter the capital until 1899.

16

Tientsin station in north-east China – an example of the cast-iron and timber platform covering typical of the earlier stations, built prior to the First World War. Apart from those in the northeast (Manchuria) most lines did not open until well into the second half of the decade. Tientsin dates from 1912.

South Australia were originally in agreement that their gauge should be 5 ft 3 in. This was the gauge put forward by the Irishman, Shields, who was the engineer of the New South Wales Railway (5 ft 3 in was the gauge finally adopted for Ireland). The problem arose when Shields departed in high dudgeon after a salary cut, and his Scots successor (on the recommendation of the then Colonial Secretary, Gladstone), selected the British 4 ft 8½ in gauge. To make matters worse, Queensland and Western Australia chose the cheaper 3 ft 6 in gauge. It was not until a century later that a continuous 4 ft 8½ in gauge trans-Australia route, from Sydney to Perth, was inaugurated.

Similar problems could have occurred in New Zealand. The first railway, the 4½-mile long Lyttleton & Christchurch, was built to Australia's 5 ft 3 in gauge, and the other promoters played about with both standard and 3 ft 6 in gauge. London soon stepped in, and required the 3 ft 6 in gauge throughout.

Japan was a comparative latecomer to the scene because of initial hostility to all things foreign. Britain was again to the fore and, arising from advice from the Minister Plenipotentiary, Sir Harry Parks, British engineers built the first line (to the metre gauge) from Tokyo to Yokohama in 1872.

But Japan is better known today for the modernity of its railways including the famous Tokaido route, with its super express trains running at speeds up to 130 mph. This is a quite separate railway from the normal state-owned 3 ft 6 in gauge system, being built to the

17

Interior of one of the first wagon-restaurant bogie cars used on the Orient-Express in 1883. In 1881 the first custom-built restaurant car was produced in Munich with walls padded in leather and ceilings painted in the Italian stucco design.

standard gauge and completely from scratch, cutting a swathe through the countryside to give Japan one of today's most up-to-date train rides.

Two of the largest systems in the world are in socialist countries, the U.S.S.R. and China. The latter country was, like Japan, equally suspicious of foreigners. It was the renowned firm of Jardine Matheson who got there first by pretending to build a road from Shanghai to Woosung, but turning it into a railway. This system began operations in 1876 but after a train hit and killed a coolie all services had to cease. After protracted negotiations the Chinese Government purchased the assets and shipped them off to Formosa, out of the way. There, in due respect to the dead, they were left to rot away. It was not until after the Sino-Japanese war in 1895 that further rails were laid.

The other colonial continent was Africa: railways here neatly grouped themselves into the four points of the compass. To the north on the Mediterranean coast, the French and British constructed and equipped railways to the standards known in Europe and to Europe's gauge of 4 ft 8½ in (1435 mm). To the east, the Italians and French dug deep into Eritrea, Somaliland, and Ethiopia with the 950-mm gauge while south of these came the vast areas of land penetrated by the Kenya and Uganda Railways to the metre gauge. In the south there is the 'Cape Gauge' of 3 ft 6 in (1067 mm) which makes up the long lines of what is now Zambia, Zimbabwe, Malawi, Mozambique and South Africa. On the west coast, Ghana, Nigeria and Angola also use the Cape Gauge. All in all there are over eight gauges of railway in Africa of which the 4 ft 8½ in gauge and the 3 ft 6 in are the most common. Eight countries in the south of Africa operate over 50 per cent of the total mileage of the continent's railways.

Egypt is the proud owner of the oldest railway system in Africa, dating from 1852 with its mainline running south from Cairo to Aswan. Once it was hoped that there could be a link from south to north – in fact the Cape to Cairo Railway was one of Cecil Rhodes's great dreams. It could have been a possibility, albeit with changes of gauge, but greed, wars, and the splintering of Africa into separate nations have put paid to this forever.

The 19th century was the time for pioneering, and with this came the advance of industrial technology, causing European nations to burst their seams. With colonial rule and business exploitation, steel tracks were laid across five huge continents. When Queen Victoria ascended to the throne, railways were in their very infancy; by the time she died in 1901 they were the life-lines of nations.

Early Train Travel

Hilaire Belloc described the early first-class railway coaches as 'a series of stage-coach insides tacked onto one another'. This was probably truer than he thought, as those early French vehicles were, in fact, three bodies mounted on a railway-wagon frame.

Such coaches were well known in England, though in the beginning they were much smaller, consisting of a road coach adapted for the railway. Omitting the very early Stockton & Darlington examples as being crude and nonstandard, the first were short-wheelbase (7-ft) coaches built for the Liverpool & Manchester Railway. Each was mounted on four 5-ft elliptical springs and there was a combined spring buffering and drawgear. This was probably the design of Henry Booth, co-entrant of the *Rocket* with the Stephensons at the 1829 Rainhill trials and inventor of the screw coupling. Like the road coach, box seats were mounted on the roof for the guards and railings were provided to contain the passengers' luggage. Inside, there were six seats upholstered in a drab brown cloth, separated by fixed wooden elbows. The three compartments were very cramped, and gave an extremely rough ride by today's standards.

Second- and third-class passengers were suffered rather than encouraged by the railways. The latter travelled in completely open boxes without roofs. In fact the Great Western needed considerable persuasion to allow such persons to travel at all, but eventually

An example of an early Liverpool & Manchester Railway first class carriage of 1830. Like the contemporary road coaches, these vehicles carried individual names as well as the company ownership. There were three compartments each containing six upholstered but hard seats; luggage was carried on the roof.

A third class carriage of the Liverpool & Manchester Railway. No refinements were available for the lower orders who had no roof, and were lucky if they had wooden benches to sit on. Most trains in the early days carried first and second class; third class was often mixed in with freight.

admitted them to open goods wagons with planks laid across. There was nothing to prevent people falling out of them, and on Christmas Eve 1841 some did, when a night goods train (suitable for cheap passengers) ran into a land slip in Sonning cutting.

Second-class passengers were treated a little better – the railways tended to think of them as the equivalent of 'outside' on a stage-coach, and thus acceptable. Fanny Kemble described her Liverpool & Manchester vehicle as a *char à banc* with seats across it.

Without a doubt the very best coaches of the 1840s were Brunel's 7-ft gauge ones belonging to the Great Western Railway. These six wheelers with their large 4-ft diameter wheels became the line's standard vehicle until the late 1870s; they were also oil lit. It is interesting to note that the road-coach builders did not suffer from the railway bonanza in the same way as the canal owners and innkeepers did. With the new and large-scale industry of railway-coach building they made a lot of money.

As a rule whenever early railways laid their tracks only rank or wealth was catered for until the middle of the 19th century. The 1850s saw a grudging raising of standards with, perhaps, a thin seat cushion accompanied by a very narrow stuffed strip running along a boarded seat back in third class and that was it. One renowned author has remarked that the disgusting habits of the proletariat in early and middle Victorian years provided an excuse for those who favoured cattle-truck standards. If there were enough pennies for railway tickets (Parliament introduced a Cheap Train Act in 1844 demanding one train in each direction on every line at a penny per mile), there could be enough for cheap drink to while away the tedium of a slow train journey. Often at the end of the ride there would be 'drunk and disorderly' offences galore. In fact around 1873 Richard Mansell of the South Eastern Railway sank iron funnels in the floor of that

Left: Queen Victoria was one of the early patrons of Britain's railways, travelling from Windsor to London and north to Balmoral. This illustration shows the interior of an early London & North Western Railway saloon.

Above: The U.S.A. led the way with bogie coaches as a short rigid wheelbase did not suit the poorly laid track. By the 1860s Pullman coaches were in operation and these set the pace for development. The standard long-distance bogie coach for many years had seats which were convertible into lying accommodation, whilst above them were wooden lockers whose lids could be lowered to give primitive upper berths. Coaches similar to this illustration were still in use for excursions and troop trains on the Canadian National Railway in the Second World War as the author well knows.

company's third-class coaches, partly to canalize the nuisance and partly to assist in 'the flushing of compartments'.

In North America the long-distance vehicles naturally improved earlier and bogie coaches appeared in regular service as the poorer track did not suit rigid short wheelbases. By 1859 the 28-year-old George Mortimer Pullman, convinced by experience that passengers would happily pay for reasonable comfort, persuaded the Chicago Alton & St. Louis Railroad to make use of his cabinet-making skills. He altered, on contract, two day cars to form convertible vehicles for overnight use. The principle was simple. At the lower level, the seats on either side of the central aisle had backs which could be lowered to form a base for mattresses. Above them was a line of bed bases which by day were hoisted flush with the ceiling. Enough customers warmed to this concept for Pullman to consider setting up on his own and building a really ambitious vehicle, resulting in the celebrated *Pioneer* of 1864. This was really excellent with an internal finish of polished black walnut with huge chandeliers for the candle lighting, genuine bedding and even marble washstands. By 1867 he had a fleet and by 1868 he introduced dining cars. Another era of rail transport had begun – in 20 years the American all-Pullman train was a fact of life.

Trains on the Great Western Railway's broad-gauge line from London to Bristol passed within sight of Windsor Castle, and it was over their tracks that the first royal journey was made – actually it was by King Friedrich Wilhelm IV of Prussia travelling to Windsor for the christening of the Princess of Wales in 1842. Later that year, on 13 June, Queen Victoria had her first ride to London by rail. Her choice of mode of travel was soon followed by the ruling families on the mainland of Europe – and by another prince, though this time a spiritual one, the Pope in 1859.

London and North-Western Express.

22

Queen Victoria was a bad sailor and used the royal yacht as little as possible, so the railway was a boon even if her journeys were somewhat circumscribed: her usual railheads were Windsor, Gosport (for Osborne House), Ballater, the Deeside terminus of the Great North of Scotland Railway (for Balmoral) and, of course, London. The Queen was very conservative in her habits as related by the Superintendent of the Line of the London & North Western Railway, G. P. Neele, over whose line she would proceed at a stately pace en route to and from Scotland. In his reminiscences Neele (who travelled in the train as his company's representative from 1843 to 1895) tells some fascinating tales.

One person he did *not* like was John Brown, and an incident of 1873 shows both this and the Queen's conservatism. Although oil lighting was available the Queen always insisted on candles in spring holders for reading. 'The Queen returned from Ballater. The journey was made as usual, with the exception that on reaching Beattock the Queen's reading lamps were wanted, and from some cause the needed candles could not be placed in the sockets. Mr. Bore tried again and again to get over the difficulty, but as time was going on he suggested that the train should proceed to Carlisle. John Brown who was with us on the ground, would not hear of this, and (as I fancy was his wont) asserted as though her Majesty had heard the suggestion "The Queen says the train shanna stir a foot till the lamps are put in" – and it had to be done.'

Twelve years later there was another great fuss en route from Windsor when the Queen discovered that gas lighting had been introduced into her saloon and requested an immediate alteration! The change had in fact been authorized by her equerry, Colonel Ponsonby, but her Majesty 'had not had the matter fully explained'.

Improvements were slower in Europe and the development of sleeper services was strangled by the tribal reluctance of governments to allow the idea of through travel. The problem was overcome in the

The Duke of Sutherland, a railway director, had his own private line running from the Highland Railway at Dunrobin. He also possessed a sumptuous saloon which he used for his more general rail journeys over the Highland Railway and other main lines. His Grace built part of the Highland Railway out of his own pocket, hence this privilege.

Below and right: The kitchen of a London & North Western Railway dining car of 1910 and the interior of a first class compartment. Note the leather-padded armrests, antimacassars, and the photographs above the seats – a practice continued up to the late 1930s. The dining car is still gas lit and of wooden construction throughout the body.

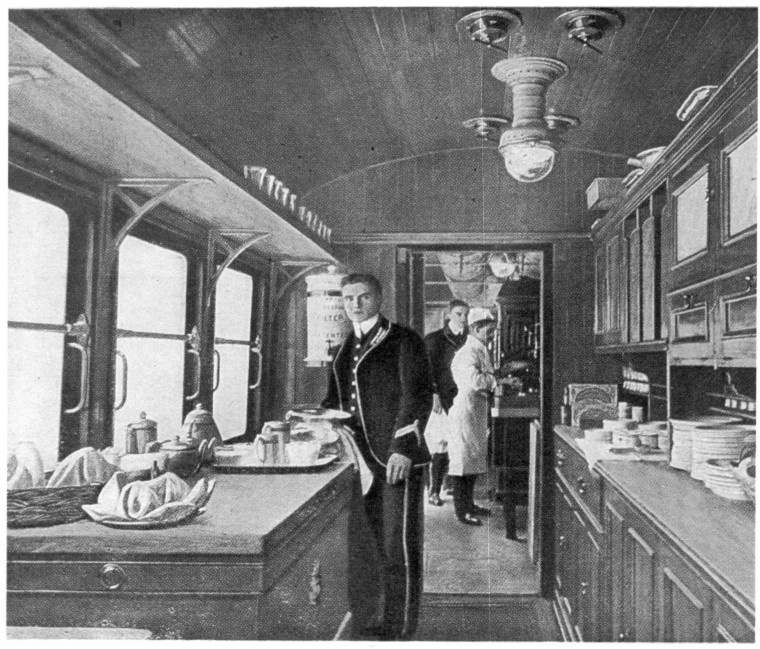

middle 1860s when an alliance of the large banking houses brought pressure to bear by making available to the railways concerned an irresistible amount of capital investment money. One of these rich banking families sent their engineer son (it is said as a penance for an indiscreet *amour*) to the U.S.A. for a while. It did not take him long to realize the potential of Pullman-type cars for Europe and the name of Georges Nagelmackers has been famous ever since. On his return to Europe in 1870 Nagelmackers sought to market his ideas, but cynical European concerns showed little interest. Success came when this astute man joined forces with a rich ex-U.S. Army engineer, Colonel William Mann, and produced what they called the '*Mann Boudoir Sleeping Cars*'. These were the first of the existing European design of sleeping vehicle. The 'game' was won after the crafty Mann persuaded King Edward VII to use a *boudoir car* for a journey to St. Petersburg. High society followed suit. Nagelmackers bought out Mann and in 1876 set up the *Compagnie Internationale des Wagons Lits et des Grandes Express Européens*, ever since known as the Wagon Lits Company. By the end of the century over 500 Wagon Lits diners and sleepers ran over routes from the French Channel ports to Russia and the borders of Turkey. By 1883 the European *train de luxe* was born when the first 'Orient Express' steamed out of Paris on 5 June.

By 1875 Britain had begun to move forward in passenger comfort and standards. James Allport of the Midland Railway persuaded a rather reluctant board of directors to abolish the old three-class structure and reduce it to two. It took a long time for the other companies to follow suit but the pressure was on. Upholstered second-class seating became third; new coaches were built including 12-wheeled bogies, though still without lavatories or corridor connections.

The Midland Railway's upgraded third class was coupled with a reduction in first-class fares which were reduced to second-class rates and this, coupled with the fact that the company was embarking on its own route to Scotland, brought competing lines up with a start. By 1887 competition was so great that the consortium of railway companies comprising the East Coast Route to Scotland (Great Northern, North Eastern and North British) announced that it was to follow the Midland's example and that, as from November of that year, their crack express, the 10 a.m. from London (King's Cross) to Edinburgh, would carry third-class passengers – an unheard of situation. Forced by this competition to follow suit, the West Coast group (London & North Western and Caledonian Railways) cut an hour from its timings between London (Euston) and Glasgow and Edinburgh from 2 June 1888. This began what, in railway history, has been known ever since as the 'race to the north', for after an uneasy truce a major contest took place in 1895. This time the goal was Aberdeen. The East Coast Route had, by this time, been shortened by the construction of bridges over the Forth and Tay rivers. The later 'race' cut *three hours* off the public timetable figures, and set yet another precedent: from then on the possibility of regular speeds of over 70 mph was recognized as being not only safe but practical, even on the standard gauge.

Left and right above: Two posters showing rival routes to Scotland, the Midland via its Settle & Carlisle extension of 1876 and the East Coast Route – a combination of the Great Northern, North Eastern and North British companies.

Below: The Midland Railway was noted for its care of passengers, and towards the end of the 19th century its coaches were renowned for their comfort. This six-wheel bogie dining car of 1906 was depicted, very properly, on one of the Company's advertising postcards.

By the year of Queen Victoria's death (1901) similar trends were apparent in Europe (where the French were excelling themselves on the Northern Railway with mile-a-minute start-to-stop trains) and in the U.S.A. where, as in Britain, competing routes vied with each other for passengers. Perhaps the American contest most similar to Britain's 'race to the north' was the competition between the New York Central and Pennsylvania RRs for the lucrative New York to Chicago traffic. On 9 May 1893 the NYC's 'Empire State Express' was said to have reached a speed of 112.5 mph behind Locomotive No. 999. Later the company confirmed that this was nearer 90 mph, but fast it certainly was. By this time Pullman cars with luxury standards for comfort and service were *de rigueur*. At the close of the century rail travel in the Western world was becoming civilized and quick with trains comprising upholstered stock, dining and sleeping facilities. Above all it was an age of railway elegance.

Below: A French railway poster produced by the Chemins de Fer de l'Est extolling the virtues of cheap tickets to the Swiss resorts of Davos and St. Moritz.

Above right: The construction of the Forth and Tay river bridges shortened the East Coast Route from Edinburgh to Aberdeen, and indirectly caused the Races of 1895 when East Coast vied with West Coast for the shortest times from London. Even today the great cantilevers of the Forth Bridge cannot fail to impress.

Right: A Clermont-Ferrand to Bordeaux express of the Paris Orleans Railway behind one of the ornate 2-4-2s of the late 1870s. Victor Fourquenot built 126 of these lovely machines, some of which ran for over 70 years. Note the magnificent Périgeux scenery, and the lavatory stock – very French, with cisterns on the carriage roofs.

Famous Express Trains

The railway races to the north triggered off a period of higher speeds in Britain and by the early Edwardian years passengers could expect to be carried at over 60 mph on most of the country's principal expresses: these included trains to the southwest as well as the more famous Scottish rivals. In fact there was also a race from Plymouth at the beginning of the century when the Great Western's 'Ocean Mail' was in competition with the London & South Western Railway for the American transatlantic mails. The epic occasion occurred on 9 May 1904 when the Churchward 4-4-0 *City of Truro* ran from Plymouth to Bristol in 2 hours 3¼ minutes, achieving a record speed of 102.3 mph down Wellington bank in Somerset. Furthermore one of William Dean's beautiful single wheelers, *Duke of Connaught*, ran from Bristol to Paddington (118.7 miles) in 99 minutes 46 seconds start to stop, an *average* speed of 80 mph. What a sight those engines must have been, speeding through the lush countryside in their dark green livery with all their brasswork sparkling in the sunshine.

An early named train. The Great Western Railway's Dutchman *climbing Wellington bank, Somerset, near Whiteball behind a Broad Gauge 4-2-2. Note the mixed gauge track. This is a late 1880s scene; complete conversion to standard gauge took place in 1892. From a painting by C. Hamilton Ellis.*

One of the great things about Britain's railways was their liveries, made up of combinations and colours of almost every hue. The London & North Western had blackberry black engines with coaches of plum and spilt milk; the Midland, red and red; the Great Eastern, royal blue and teak; even the little Midland & Great Northern vied with the London, Brighton & South Coast Railway with engines of yellowy brown – the LBSC called it Stroudley's improved engine green!

Locomotives were often named, as were the crack expresses; *Saint Benedict* could be found at the head of the 'Cornish Riviera Express' on the Great Western, or *Thunderer* on the North Western's 'Corridor' to Scotland. These named trains began their lives in the first decade of the century but it was in the interwar years that they became household words. Every boy (and most men) knew what time the 'Royal Scot' left Euston, the 'Flying Scotsman' King's Cross or the 'Cornish Riviera' Paddington. There were other names, too, which caught the imagination, the 'Atlantic Coast Express', the 'Brighton Belle', the 'Thames Clyde Express' and the 'Norfolkman'. In later years there were the speed trains such as GWR's 'Cheltenham Flyer' – the world's fastest train until the coming of the LNER and LMS streamliners in the shape of the 'Silver Jubilee', the 'Coronation' and the 'Coronation Scot'.

Facsimile Flying Scotsman *of 1888. In 1938 the LNER brought Patrick Stirling's Great Northern Railway 8-ft single wheeler No. 1 out of York Museum for the 50th anniversary of the Race to the North. This painting by M. Secretan shows the train leaving King's Cross with a typical period train of East Coast Joint Stock.*

Looking at these high-speed trains of the 1930s one can see names galore. On the LMS there was the 'Royal Scot', and the later in the morning departures from Euston included the 'Mancunian', the 'Lancastrian' and, in the afternoon the 'Comet' to Liverpool. Dull two-hour expresses to Birmingham were unnamed until the coming of British Railways who then introduced the 'Midlander'.

The LNER had its 'West Riding Pullman', 'Queen of Scots Pullman' and 'Harrogate Pullman'; the Great Western its 'Cornish Riviera Limited' and 'Torbay Express'; while the Southern gloried in the 'Golden Arrow' carrying passengers to Dover and the Channel Ports.

Europe's best-known train, indeed perhaps the world's, is the 'Orient Express', though it was never by any means Europe's fastest. Germany held the record in the mid-1930s with the 'Flying Hamburger' and in France the highest maximum speeds were obtained on the Paris-Le Havre route, but one of the super luxury trains, the 'Nord Express' carrying through-sleeping cars from Riga and Warsaw had some very high-speed running. Other European super trains included the famous 'Golden Arrow', carrying in its formation not only the Calais-Paris Pullmans but also sleepers for the 'Blue Train' and the 'Simplon Orient' cars for Trieste and Istanbul. Another French 'star turn' was the 'Sud Express' between Paris and the Spanish frontier with a northbound timing of six hours 25 minutes

Examples of British express train liveries in the pre-grouping era, that is, prior to 1923. The blue Claud Hamilton class 4-4-0 is leaving Liverpool Street station London with the Norfolk Coast Express. Note the use of red in the lining and to show off the engine's coupling rods. The brown London, Brighton & South Coast Atlantic is leaving the capital's Victoria station with the 1921 Southern Belle to Brighton. Note the use of buffer beam route codes peculiar to this railway.

Right: One of Henry Ivatt's large Great Northern Atlantics at the head of the Harrogate Pullman *in the 1920s.*

Below: The Royal Scot of the LMS on its way northwards picking up water over troughs on the West Coast main line. The locomotive is No. 6117 Welsh Guardsman, *a Royal Scot class 4-6-0 in its original condition without smoke deflectors.*

between Bordeaux and Paris, allowing recovery time from the late starts from the Spanish connections. During this period Europe's Pullmans came under the same direction as the Wagon Lits services and such trains were truly luxurious, as were the German 'Eidelweiss' and 'Rheingold' Pullmans.

In North America named trains were also everyday practice on the trunk lines; even as far back as the 1900s the New York Central had its 'Empire State Express' and that train of trains the 'Twentieth Century Limited', although almost equally high marks must go to the competition, the Pennsylvania Railroad's 'Broadway Limited'. Like the European *trains de luxe*, supplementary charges were levelled to cover the special amenities on the flyers. For many years each train

made the New York-Chicago journey in 20 hours, but by 1935 this had been reduced to 17 with overall speeds including every stop, of 56.4 mph for the 'Century' and 53 mph for the 'Broadway' – for a journey of nearly a thousand miles.

Next in line came the streamline era with the 'Hiawathas' running from Chicago to Milwaukee, originally with streamlined Atlantic locomotives at 68 mph start to stop, and the famous 'Zephyrs' on the Burlington – pioneer diesel units in 1934. A new form of motive power entered the express passenger train arena in a permanent form.

The Canadian railways have never lagged behind in public esteem though in truth, the transcontinentals were scarcely expresses. The Canadian Pacific's 'Trans-Canada Limited' with its attendant comforts compared favourably with a hotel on wheels; included were a library and a solarium. The rival, Canadian National's 'Continental Limited', was a train of equal renown. Much more like an express was the CNR's 'International Limited' which ran from Montreal, Toronto and Hamilton to Detroit using the Great Trunk Western (the U.S.A. subsidiary) after crossing the border at Windsor.

Right: The Orient Express in the 1960s when it was very much in decline and seen here in Yugoslavia behind a State Railways Pacific. At that time there were but two Wagons Lits sleepers making the whole journey from Paris to Athens (four days a week) and to Istanbul (three days a week). There were dining cars only in France, Switzerland and Turkey. For one and a half days passengers had to forage for themselves.

Above: The French section of the Golden Arrow behind one of the all brown Nord four cylinder compound 'Super Pacifics'. Note the all-Pullman Wagons Lits coaches. The English version of the train from London (Victoria) to Dover was also an all-Pullman affair.

A Paddington to Birmingham, Wolverhampton express nears the summit of Hatton bank Warwickshire with a down express in the late 1920s. Note the red locomotive headlamps, typical of the Great Western Railway, and the third track on the right which is a goods only line used to contain slow freight traffic climbing this hilly section of the route. The locomotive is No. 6001 King Edward VII.

Great train no more. The erstwhile Night Ferry Wagon Lits sleeping car train connecting London with Paris via a cross-Channel train ferry. Special Wagons Lits sleeping cars were needed to fit the more restricted British loading gauge. This was the only time that the brown uniformed Wagons Lits attendants were ever seen in Britain. The locomotives are two of the Southern Railway's L1 class built in 1926.

The French 'Blue Train' was luxurious enough but some thousands of miles away in South Africa there was (and still is) another 'Blue Train' which makes an even longer journey – 956 miles from Johannesburg to Cape Town. This South African train uses the Cape Gauge of 3 ft 6 in and began life in 1923 as the 'Union Express', requiring a first-class fare with a 50 per cent supplement, and has always been popular. In 1940 new, all-steel rolling stock was introduced with blue coach exteriors and, as with the French service, the popular title became the 'Blue Train'.

Not to be outdone by Europe, North America and Africa, the Far East also has had its named trains. Some of the best known existed in India and included the various 'Mails'. The 'Bombay Mail' and the 'Delhi Mail', for example, consisted of special coaches with ventilating fans and baths, with their attendant vehicles for native servants.

Australia was well to the fore in express-train running in the 1930s but as each state had its own gauge, through-running was out of the question. Thus, in travelling from, say, Melbourne to Sydney, passengers had to change trains at Albury. Trains consisted of compartment, saloon, parlour and sleeper stock, with restaurant cars. The year 1917 saw the opening of the transcontinental line across the desert between Port Augusta in South Australia and Kalgoorlie in Western Australia, and here, too, lounge cars, showers and a writing room were innovations.

The Second World War put an end to the speedy and luxurious trains of Britain, Europe and North America – national needs had to come first. Sadly the superb trains died, and although speed eventually returned, absolute luxury did not. The height of records for steam, the London & North Eastern Railway's momentary 126 mph with its A4 Pacific *Mallard* on 3 July 1938, was never to be beaten. Railways everywhere came under increasing and intensifying strain. The aftermath of war found Britain's and Europe's mainline railways in poor shape. The result in Britain was nationalization from 1 January 1948 and in Europe there were gigantic reconstruction programmes. Slowly (within a decade) train speeds improved and efforts were made to improve standards and reliability. Named trains came back with British Western Region's 'Bristolian' taking the speed laurels. Naming of trains once again became *de rigueur* for the major expresses – new names included the 'Midlander', 'Merchant Ven-

The famous 20th Century Limited *all-Pullman train at the beginning of the century behind a high wheeling Atlantic. It was then covering the 980 miles between New York and Chicago in 18 hours.*

A through train from Paris to Italy emerging from the Gotthard tunnel in the days of steam. Double heading was de rigueur *over this heavily graded but very important international route.*

turer', 'Cathedrals Express' and 'Waverley'. All imitated prewar patterns and all were steam-hauled. But it was to be diesel power which led to a more efficient (though less romantic) future. This really began in Europe with the arrival of the TEE – the Trans Europe Express.

The inspiration for these luxury intercity, interstate expresses came from Holland, and by the mid-1950s six countries – France, West Germany, Luxembourg, Holland, Switzerland and Italy – embraced the principle with the general acceptance that these TEE trains would be diesel multiple units, though, in the event, in later years they became predominantly locomotive hauled. It was a first-class dream which never really worked out as planned, though without the TEEs of yesterday, today's comfortable high-speed trains might never have

A mail train leaving Bombay in the 1920s behind one of the BESA 4-6-0s of the Great Indian Peninsular Railway. Note the wide 5 ft 6 in gauge and the white anti-glare coaches.

Right: An early postcard showing the St. Petersburg (Leningrad) to Moscow express crossing the flat countryside in wintry weather prior to the First World War.

Below: The Inter-State Express connecting Melbourne (Victoria) and Sydney (New South Wales) in the 1920s. The train is made up of saloon, parlour and restaurant cars plus an observation coach.

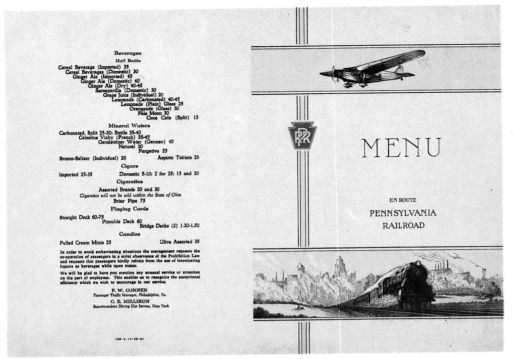

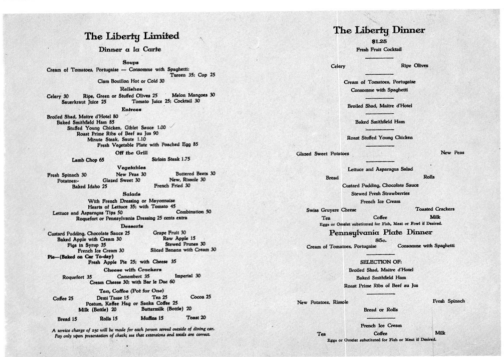

arrived. Problems in the path of the dream were mainly national. For instance, there could not be an overall inclusive ticket including meals because Wagons Lits, the German Mitropa organization and the Swiss catering company protested that it would be administratively too difficult to harmonize the prices.

In the U.S.A. the problems were different. Although the railways were heavily used and worn down by wartime traffic, passenger services over the long distances concerned were more affected by the advent of air competition which was well-organized and compared favourably in price. The once 'Great Trains' became 'Great Trains No More'. By the late 1950s the difficulties had become acute, and by 1958 the 'Twentieth Century Limited's all-Pullman tradition ceased with the introduction of sleeping coaches and reclining seats at second-class prices. By 1970 the train had made its last run and in the same year Penn Central, the conglomerate made up of two old companies which had not been able to survive on their own, finally went bankrupt.

Left: Almost the end of an era. The Southern Pacific's Daylight observation car at San Francisco in 1952.

Another famous train to go was the Santa Fe's 'Super Chief' which had been introduced in 1937 as the first-ever diesel-hauled all-Pullman streamliner. The train initially had created a tremendous stir by cutting over 15 hours off the journey-time from Chicago to Los Angeles. The 'Super Chief' gave such comfort and superb food that the Santa Fe refused to allow its name to continue on the revival service now running under AMTRAK. In its heyday the 'Super Chief' had carried a barber service and even offered news bulletins and stock reports, providing passengers with its own specially headed notepaper.

One of the advanced ideas which permeated North American high-quality trains from the 1950s onwards was the use of 'dome cars', beginning with the dome diners constructed for Union Pacific's 'City of Los Angeles' in 1955. These were later followed by incorporating panoramic lounges which extended the full length of the coach, while Southern Pacific produced some three-quarter-length vehicles for its 'Daylight' streamliners. As the 1950s rolled on, more and more companies followed suit soon. The dome-car innovation became the norm.

Above: Steam's Indian Summer. The Merchant Venturer *passes through Swindon station on its way from London to Bristol around 1960. The Castle class 4-6-0 No. 5071* Spitfire's *coaches are resplendent in the old Great Western Railway's livery of chocolate and cream.*

39

When Steam Was King

Just over 150 years ago the world's first public railway, the Liverpool & Manchester, was opened to traffic; its engineer was George Stephenson and his prize-winning locomotive, *Rocket*, was to become famous worldwide. Two features of the new *Rocket* were innovations – and important ones. First, the boiler was multi-tubular in that it contained a considerable number of small flues which provided a much greater heating surface than one large equivalent. Second, its cylinders exhausted their steam to a chimney through a smokebox by means of a blast pipe; this created a partial vacuum which, in its turn, pulled air from the fire via the tubes, causing new air to rush in and draw this to a fierce heat. Because it automatically links heat production with need, this system has remained in use right up to the present day.

In the same year, 1830, a new type of locomotive appeared on the Liverpool & Manchester Railway – the inside-cylindered *Planet*. An obvious change was the placing of the cylinders at the front end thus giving better weight distribution. In addition, fitting these between the frames instead of outside helped to make the little engine more stable with the thrust of the piston rods on a more central line. Similar engines were built elsewhere in the world, including one in the U.S.A. by Matthias Baldwin, the father of the famous locomotive building works carrying his name.

The present-day replica of Stephenson's Rocket *is a fully working example of 1830 practice. During the last few years it has toured the world, including exhibitions in the U.S.A., Australia and Japan. It is shown here with America's* Tom Thumb *(also of 1830 and on loan from the Smithsonian Museum) at Sacramento in May 1981.*

A replica of the Broad Gauge North Star *built by Stephenson for the infant Great Western Railway in 1837. This was the only successful locomotive used by the railway prior to the construction of Daniel Gooch's famous Firefly class of 2-2-2 in 1840. Once at Swindon locomotive works, it is now in the town's Railway Museum.*

Overleaf: The Baltimore & Ohio Railroad's William Mason *is a typical example of mid-19th century American railroad practice. This ornate 4-4-0 type was first put on the rails by Thomas Rogers in 1852 and lasted in normal service for nigh on a hundred years, dominating railway operations in North America for over a generation.*

Below: The Liverpool & Manchester Railway 0-4-2 Lion *of 1838. This historic locomotive was rescued in 1920 and restored and is now in the Merseyside County Museum, Liverpool.*

With heavier loads to be moved, the problem of power loomed quickly into prominence. By 1838 the Leeds firm of Todd Kitson & Laird had produced the 0-4-2 *Lion*. This design was another step forward: the coupling together of the driving wheels gave additional power as adhesion was spread over two axles. One of the disadvantages suffered by the pioneer railway engineers was the availability of materials: there was no steel at that time; and the wrought-iron rails, axles and boiler shells had little strength compared with today's products.

The next 20 years saw considerable development in design, and locomotives began to emerge in the more familiar pattern of later

The German firm of Borsig in Berlin built this Swedish Beyer Peacock-like 2-4-0 No. 198 Breda in 1875. The polished brass dome and copper-capped chimney are typical of this age of locomotive development. Like the British, the Germans had several successful locomotive building firms who competed for export orders, thus extending the spheres of trading influence.

years. One of the well-known experimental designs was that of Thomas Crampton whose engines made their mark in railway history. Crampton put his driving axle behind the boiler which enabled him to set it low, keeping down the centre of gravity, but there was a drawback in that the adhesive weight which could be applied to that single pair of wheels was small. Nevertheless, over 300 engines to his design ran over Europe's railways, mainly in France. They were ideal for fast, light trains. Crampton's engines were very beautiful and built to high engineering principles (for example, he was one of the first to apply proper balancing to the reciprocating motion). One of his locomotives is preserved in working order, a 4-2-0 of the Eastern Railway of France.

Another engineer of considerable note was Daniel Gooch of the Great Western Railway. Gooch took charge of Isambard Kingdom Brunel's 7 ft 0¼ in gauge locomotive development and followed the six-wheeled 2-2-2 *North Star* with a series of beautiful engines, all of which had appropriate names beginning with the word fire. These included *Fire Fly, Fire King* and *Fire Brand*. These 1840-built machines were fully capable of running at speeds approaching 60 mph. Gooch later developed a series of 4-2-2s and these, too, have been long remembered. They hauled the Great Western expresses for many years, achieving high running speeds, as recorded by the historian E. L. Ahrons who timed *Lightning* down Wellington bank near Taunton in Somerset at just over 81 mph.

By the mid-1850s some standardization was becoming apparent. For example, Britain was using 4-2-2s and 2-4-0s for fast passenger working with 0-6-0s for freight; Europe took to larger locomotives with 4-4-0s introduced into Austria by 1848. But it was in the United States of America that this wheel arrangement became the norm for many years; in fact in wheel nomenclature, the 4-4-0, is known as the 'American'. It lasted until it was superseded by the 'ten wheelers' – 4-6-0s – in the 1880s.

One of the American engineers to make his mark was Thomas Rogers of New Jersey and it was his engine, the 4-4-0 *General* of 1855, which became famous during the Civil War when it was hijacked by Union soldiers who had penetrated behind Confederate lines, the resulting adventures becoming part of American folklore. One of Rogers's achievements was his application of Stephenson's link motion which allowed the expansive use of steam – a very important development. The use of a bogie which led the locomotive round curves was to become a feature of locomotive design the world over.

Right: One of the distinctive 2-4-2s of class 121 built for the French Paris, Lyons & Mediterranean Railway from 1876 picking up the Riviera Express from the Italian State Railways at Ventimiglia around the turn of the century. This was a classic French design and one of these locomotives is now preserved in the National Railway Museum at Mulhouse.

The U.S.A., in contrast to European development, saw the rise of independent locomotive manufacturers who supplied virtually standard engines to order. In Britain (and Europe) the larger companies built their own machines to the design of the Mechanical Engineer concerned.

By the late 1870s more attention was being paid to the efficiency of locomotives and one of the ideas promulgated was compounding. The principle involved the re-use of steam by taking the initial exhaust (high pressure) into a second set of cylinders (low pressure) thus using the steam twice. This was explored in the 1880s by Francis Webb, Chief Mechanical Engineer to the London & North Western Railway, who tried two outside high-pressure cylinders with a huge inside low-pressure one. It was not a success. S. W. Johnson of the Midland Railway introduced a system of a single high-pressure cylinder and

Below: A painting of one of the F.W. Webb-designed 2-2-2-0 compound locomotives built for the London & North Western Railway in 1889. The huge low pressure inside cyclinder drove the front pair of wheels whilst the two high pressure cylinders were coupled to the rear pair. The system was not a success.

One of Britain's exports to its Empire. A Beyer Peacock 3 ft 6 in gauge 2-6-0 of 1890 as South Australia Railways No. 97 at Peterborough in March 1964. South Australia used the Irish gauge of 5 ft 3 in for its main lines, but this section from Port Pirie to Peterborough is part of a large 3 ft 6 in network.

two low-pressure cylinders in 1902; it worked, and engines of this type, though improved, continued to be built into the 1920s.

Compounding was not popular in England and scarcely used in North America, but in Europe, especially in France, the idea took hold. One of the most famous designers to use this principle was Alfred de Glehn who joined with Gaston de Bousquet of the Northern Railway of France to develop an arrangement of compounding which was to become known worldwide and, what is more, to stand the test of time. Right up to the end of steam in the mid-20th century, French express locomotives were de Glehn compounds. One reason for the success of compounding in France was the fact that all French drivers were skilled mechanics who had been through the workshops as part of their training. Indeed *mechanicien* is the French word for driver. This was in direct contrast to most other countries and certainly contrary to British and American practice where drivers were drivers, and that was that. Of course the rudiments of 'how it works' were an important part of their training and knowledge, but no more. As a result, French enginemen knew the whys and wherefores and were keen to handle their locomotives efficiently, and this combined with coal-saving and timekeeping bonuses made compounding work.

By the turn of the century the simple American outside-cylinder 4-6-0 had proved its worth and was in use over most of the continent. Meanwhile, in Britain, loads were becoming heavier (because of corridor coaches and dining cars) and, at the same time, higher speeds were being demanded by competitively minded managements so more powerful locomotives were needed. Churchward of the Great Western Railway laid down the foundations of modern British motive power by purchasing three de Glehn compound 4-4-2s from France and run-

Above: One of the world's great locomotive classes, the Nord Railway's de Glehn Atlantic of 1910. These French 4-4-2 compounds had four cylinders (inside low pressure, outside high pressure). This example, No. 2670, is seen as restored in the French National Railway Museum at Mulhouse.

ning them side by side with his simple 4-4-2s and 4-6-0s. Out of it all came the best of both worlds – a combination of American and French practice resulting in the standard GWR two-cylindered Saints and four-cylindered Stars whose design, if modified, was to last until the end of steam in Britain.

About the same time another important locomotive development took place, this time in India – the advent of the first British Engineering Standards Association (BESA) heavy locomotives. One in particular, the 'Heavy 4-6-0' was a very successful engine indeed and members of the class were built as late as 1950. To see one of these engines at speed through the countryside in the 1980s is like being transported backwards in time. India also uses representatives of American practice, particular inspiration stemming from Baldwin's of Philadelphia in the form of WP Pacifics.

Another classic design from Europe was the Prussian P8 class 4-6-0 of 1906 (Royal Prussian Union Railway). This two-cylinder engine needed some modification before enjoying the success known to enthusiasts today, but once the bugs were ironed out of it, the class was built in large numbers, many for export. Nearly 4,000 were

Overleaf: The Royal Prussian Union Railway 4-6-0 of 1906 proved to be an extremely successful design. One of Romanian State Railways engines, No. 230.083, takes a local train north of Bucharest in the late 1960s.

eventually constructed in Germany and other nearby countries. They lasted in West Germany until 1975 but examples continue to operate in Poland and Romania well into the 1980s.

The end of King Edward VII's reign not only saw an age of tremendous railway elegance, it also ushered in one of the finest British inside-cylinder 4-4-0s ever to be built, the George the Fifth class, designed by C. J. Bowen-Cooke for the London & North Western Railway. These engines were built at Crewe from scratch (exactly that – the works was a complete entity from foundry to erecting shop) from 1910: they were the first North Western engines to be superheated (Schmidt), had piston valves with Joy valve gear and thought nothing of train loads up to 400 tons on the West Coast mainline. A few years later Bowen-Cooke produced his inside-cylinder 4-6-0, Prince of Wales class and later, the four-cylinder Claughton 4-6-0 which was his *pièce de resistance*. Although the Prince of Wales engines were capable of extremely hard work, lasting with the 'Georges' just into nationalization, it was the 4-4-0 which was the legend. Sadly the class went to its last rest only a few years before the British Transport Commission decided to set up a Railway Museum.

Sadly, no London & North Western Railway 4-4-0 or 4-6-0 was ever preserved. The final LNWR express class to be built (in 1913) was C.J. Bowen-Cooke's Claughton – a four-cylinder simple 4-6-0. This painting shows an LNWR train of the immediate pre First World War years behind one of these locomotives in the spotless external condition of the period.

The year 1914 saw the emergence of another legendary locomotive class, the Pennsylvania Railroad's K4 Pacific. In all, some 425 of these efficient machines were built over a period of 14 years. They were used on the railroad's principal express services, including the Broadway Limited. *This photograph shows a train headed by a K4 passing Fort Wayne, Indiana.*

*The Great
Northern
Railway's A1 class
three-cylinder
Pacific, designed
by Nigel Gresley
and entering
service in 1922,
has become famous
through the name*
Flying Scotsman.
*These 4-6-2s, later
designated class A3
by the London &
North Eastern
Railway, handled
the fastest East
Coast main line
expresses until the
coming of the
streamlined A4
Pacifics in 1935.
No. 2550* Galtee
More *takes a train
of LNER teak
coaches north in
the 1920s.*

*Rivals (and
successful ones at
that) to the LNER
A3 Pacifics were
the Great Western
Railway's Castle
class four-cylinder
4-6-0s, dating
from 1923. Built
from then on until
early British
Railways time in
1950, the Castles
handled most of the
GWR expresses
including the 1930s
World's Fastest
Train – the*
Cheltenham Flyer
*– and the post-
Second World
War* Bristolian.
*The first of its
class, No. 4073*
Caerphilly Castle
*(now preserved in
London's Science
Museum), is seen
here in the 1920s.*

Meanwhile, in the U.S.A., loads were also growing heavier and intercity services such as the 'Broadway Limited' on the Pennsylvania Railroad demanded fast schedules with good timekeeping; here, too, stronger motive power was essential. The company was the only one in the U.S.A. to set up its own locomotive testing plant (at Altoona). (There were others in Britain and in France.) The idea behind this was to be able to roadtest a locomotive on rollers so that the instruments concerned could pick up the vital happenings within the locomotive itself. In this way theoretical calculations in design were checked against actual performance under practical but works conditions. Such tests were applied to one of the company's most famous locomotives, the K4 Pacific of 1914 – yet another legendary locomotive. Such was their success that they handled all the Pennsylvania's express passenger trains (outside the electrified area) until after the Second World War, although heavy loads at times resulted in double heading. Like the Great Western Railway with its 1930s 'Cheltenham Flyer', the Pennsylvania's 'Detroit Arrow' was an interwar record breaker: in 1934 it was the fastest train in the world covering the 64 miles from Plymouth to Fort Wayne with an average speed of $75\frac{1}{2}$ mph.

The First World War saw a temporary halt to locomotive development but by the early 1920s two other designs of considerable note appeared on the scene: one in Britain, the other in France. They were the Great Northern Railway's (soon to become the LNER) A1 class (later A3) Pacific of 1922 and the Nord's Super Pacific of 1923. Of these LNER No. 4472 *Flying Scotsman* has become one of the world's best known locomotives. These three-cylinder engines were also record breakers with No. 2750 *Papyrus* named after a racehorse) touching 108 mph on a high-speed run from Newcastle to London in 1935. Later LNER Pacifics were fitted with corridor tenders to allow crew changing on the nonstop run from London to Edinburgh.

A number of locomotive types and classes which lasted to the very last years of the steam era first saw the light of day during the 1920s.

The British mixed traffic 4-6-0 is epitomized by Sir William Stanier's class 5 4-6-0 of 1934. These ubiquitous two-cylinder engines were used all over the LMS system and were later

built by British Railways and given an even wider route coverage. In BR black, No. 45407 stands by the coaling stage at Carnforth in Lancashire.

These included Britain's A3 Pacifics (LNER), Royal Scots (LMS), King Arthurs (Southern), and the Castles and Kings of the Great Western. Of these the Castles, a logical development of Churchward's four-cylinder Stars, proved long lived, economical and thoroughly efficient engines; one, No. 4079 *Pendennis Castle*, went to the LNER (an exchange visit with an A1) and beat the host company's engines on their own home ground. No. 7029 *Clun Castle* (actually built under the auspices of British Railways) took the speed record over the Plymouth to Bristol route from *City of Truro* as late as May 1964. From 1923 until the end of steam on the Western Region, Castles

were seen at work. Not that the Kings' performances could be ignored – far from it – but because of their heavy axle-loading, these engines were generally limited to London-Plymouth and London-Wolverhampton via Birmingham routes in GWR days.

Another class to be constructed in the 1920s was a further American classic – the New York Central J3a class 4-6-4 – the famous Hudson. These locomotives worked the crack '20th Century Limited' against the Pennsylvania's K4s on the competing 'Broadway Limited'. The Hudsons worked most of the NYC expresses and even penetrated into Canada (Toronto) over a joint section of line with the Canadian Pacific known as the Toronto, Hamilton and Buffalo Railway.

One of the A4s, No. 4468 Mallard, is the holder of the world's speed record for a steam locomotive, 126 mph down Stoke bank on 3 July 1938. A commemorative plaque has since been carried on the locomotive which is now preserved in the National Railway Museum, York.

Right: In 1935 Nigel Gresley introduced his streamlined A4 class Pacifics to the LNER. This was the beginning of the late 1930s streamline era when the locomotives were originally used to haul the Silver Jubilee *and* Coronation *expresses. Later, the class headed most of the East Coast principal trains. Liveries ranged from silver to garter blue to green. Preserved in garter blue is No. 4498, named after its designer* Sir Nigel Gresley. *Note the conventional smokebox door hidden behind the wedge-shaped streamlined front.*

The 1930s saw some of the final development of steam power, certainly as far as really high-speed trains were concerned. By then road competition was beginning to be felt badly, and in an attempt to fight back, the railways introduced the streamliners. In Britain these included the LNER's 'Silver Jubilee' and 'Coronation' expresses on the East Coast route, with the 'Coronation Scot' on the West Coast. To head the trains the companies introduced new locomotives; the LNER used Gresley's super A4 Pacifics in silver or garter blue, and the LMS employed Coronation class Pacifics in blue and silver or red and gold. The A4s were all streamlined; the LMS Pacifics were built both streamlined and as conventional locomotives. France also introduced a limited number of streamliners, as did the Germans on the 'Flying Hamburger'. Across the Atlantic in Canada and the U.S.A., streamlined or semi-streamlined engines were also hard at work. Canada had 4-6-4s on the Canadian Pacific and the Canadian National Railways used a few 4-8-4s.

Perhaps the best known of the American streamlined and semi-streamlined engines were those built for the Milwaukee RR's 'Hiawathas' in the form of 4-4-2s (class A) and 4-6-4s (class F7), and the Southern Pacific's class GS 4-8-4s used on the 'Daylight' expresses between Los Angeles and San Francisco. These big oil burners eventually spread to all parts of the SP system and the first was not withdrawn from service until as late as 1954. One, No. 4449, has been preserved in operable condition resplendent in its 'Daylight' colours.

The Canadian
Pacific Royal
Hudson class 4-6-4
was built in 1937
as motive power for
its transcontinental
passenger trains.
One direct result
was the time saved
by reducing the
number of
locomotive changes
needed to cross
Canada from 14 to
nine. For a short
few months in 1931
this class hauled
the fastest train in
the world, the
Royal York *from
Montreal to
Toronto, until
eclipsed by the
Great Western's*
Cheltenham
Flyer. *No. 2860 is
among those saved
from the breakers
yards and this
engine now works
on regular tourist
services over the
British Columbia
Railway between
Vancouver and
Squamish.*

The 1930s also saw the wider use of the British common-use mixed-traffic locomotives as exemplified by the earlier GWR Hall class but epitomized by Stanier's LMS class 5 4-6-0. Stanier had come from the Great Western with a remit to modernize and standardize LMS power. The 'Black Fives', as they were known, became the most numerous and most versatile of any class on the railway; they were capable of handling anything from an express to a freight train. As time went on these engines could be found in every corner of the system, and on nationalization they were successfully used in other regions, including the West Highland line from Glasgow to Fort William where they generally hunted in pairs replacing the K2 class LNER 2-6-0s and sounding the death knell of the old North British Railway Glen class 4-4-0s, built for the route. They hauled the last steam trains in regular service on British Railways tracks. Other common users, built later, which gave particularly outstanding service in mainland Europe were the German 2-10-0 'Kriegslok' locomotives, constructed in their thousands during the Second World War. These engines have ended up as far away as Turkey and are still at work there and in Eastern Europe. The French also were particularly fortunate in the 2-8-2 type, again built in large numbers, provided by American and Canadian manufacturers for the vital postwar reconstruction programme. The 1-4-1Rs did for French Railways what the Black Fives did for the LMS and British Railways. They were truly magnificent engines, simple and sturdy.

Steam motive power developed country by country to fit in with individual operating requirements, terrain by terrain. The needs of the less developed areas of the world were supplied by the big

Another Canadian giant is the CNR class U 4-8-4, again used for cross-Canada trains. Dating from 1936 these fine engines eventually totalled 203 and could be seen anywhere between Halifax and the West Coast, some even working in the U.S.A. on the CNR's subsidiary, the Grand Trunk Western. No. 6218 is seen here crossing a trestle bridge in Quebec.

Garratt articulated locomotives have been the mainstay of Southern Africa's steam services for many years. South African Railways have now pensioned off their fleet but 4-6-4 + 4-6-4 and 4-8-2 + 2-8-4 locomotives are still at work in Zimbabwe. This photograph shows a selection of this type sitting in the locomotive shed at Bulawayo in 1971.

locomotive manufacturers, often in competition with each other. British companies, such as North British, Armstrong Whitworth and Beyer-Peacock met the demands of the Colonies and Empire; American firms such as Baldwin and the American Locomotive Company (Alco) penetrated many areas; Germany's Henschel did the same. The Americans were, somewhat naturally, extremely successful in South America but their rugged, simple locomotives performed well everywhere.

One design, albeit a specialized one, enters the scene here – the Beyer Garratt. H. W. Garratt combined his invention with the skills of the locomotive-building firm of Beyer Peacock of Manchester to produce a locomotive type which was (and still is) quite unique, and ideally suited for railways where a considerable power output was required, combined with relatively light axle-loading. The Garratt engine is in effect two in one: two conventional units of a given wheel arrangement are used back to back as bogies with a boiler cradle slung between them. The water tank and fuel bunkers are carried over the units. The whole engine is not only strong but capable of running at comparatively high speeds, the boiler and cab unit moving inwards like a bowstring within a bow, countering the overturning effect of centrifugal force when running round sharp curves. Garratts have seen most of their service in Africa but have enjoyed considerable success in South America and Australia. They had a limited use in Britain and did not come onto the locomotive scene in Europe or North America where the Mallet articulated locomotives were more popular. All of the Garratts at work today are in Southern Africa, mostly in Zimbabwe and Angola, though there are some miniscule examples on the South African narrow gauge.

Although British Railways designed and produced a series of standard locomotives in the early 1950s, among which the 9F class 2-10-0 probably carried the honours, it was in Europe, the U.S.A. and the Far East that the laurels really lay. Dieselization came early to North America, but steam's final fling produced some magnificent machines including the Union Pacific's FEF2 class 4-8-4 of 1939 – FEF standing for four-eight-four. These were numbered in the 800 series and the final batch of ten came out in 1944 as FEF3s. These came from Alco and were the last steam locomotives built for UP. They were superb machines, giving high-speed performances up to the design limit of 110 mph. One, No. 844, is preserved in working order.

Other railroads, including the Pennsylvania with its 4-4-4-4 duplex engines, came up with modern designs. Of these the Norfolk & Western Railway's class J 4-8-4 came as near to fighting off the diesel invasion as any. But the Union Pacific had, by far, the biggest engine of them all. This was their 1942-built Challenger 4-6-6-4, the most powerful locomotive that ever handled express passenger trains. It was an articulated locomotive, in other words there was a hinge in the middle along the lines of a Mallet but it was a simple not a compound. To see and hear one of these engines at work running at speeds of up to 70 mph between Salt Lake City and Los Angeles was to witness the ultimate in steam power. Fortunately, one has been preserved in working order and can be seen on special trains from time to time.

France also produced a magnificent machine, the SNCF's 2-4-1P, a 4-8-2 based on a Paris Lyons Mediterranean Railway design and a four-cylinder compound. These 1948 André Chapelon engines could load up to 950 tons, though their normal trains were more in the region of 800. To travel behind one of these exquisite machines over the main line to Clermont Ferrand in the late 1960s was a thrilling experience, a really wonderful Indian Summer for Europe's steam power.

The world's biggest steam passenger locomotive was the Union Pacific Railroad's Challenger class 4-6-6-4 of 1942. These huge locomotives were four-cylinder simples and 64 of them were eventually built for use over the main line to Los Angeles. No. 3985 has been preserved in working order and is used from time to time on enthusiast specials.

Left: Two of China's representatives of modern locomotive power. On the left is a QJ 2-10-2, on the right a DFH₃ diesel hydraulic, seen at Changchun locomotive depot, Manchuria, in 1980. On the very right, in the distance, is an SL class Pacific.

Above: One of South African Railways class 25 4-8-4, built from 1953 as condensing engines. In 1969 the condensing engines were still hard at work, as can be seen by this train headed southbound from Beisiespoort, between de Aar and Hutchinson.

But today one has to travel to the Far East for big steam. No longer do the Soviet Union's P36 class 4-8-4s roll the Trans-Siberian train eastwards for electrification has taken over, but in China they are still building. To the northwest of Peking lies the Datong steam locomotive factory, and here, only 20 miles from Inner Mongolia, 7,000 workers produce around 250 new steam locomotives every year. Like those built at Crewe, Datong's engines begin in the factory foundry. These are the Qianjin (Forward) class of 2-10-2s, simple but very strong two-cylinder locomotives. They work throughout China mainly on freights, but also on local passenger services. To see QJs rolling over one of the huge river bridges, heading their normal 3,000-ton freight trains, or pounding up the bank and under the tunnel below China's Great Wall are sights and sounds now forgotten in the West.

Overleaf: Steam locomotives are still being built at Datong in the People's Republic of China. These comprise the QJ (Forward) class 2-10-2. Freight trains regularly load to over 3,000 tons. No. 773 is seen here at Wuhan shed in May 1983.

Trains in the West

The present generation of railwaymen, faced with cut-throat competition from car, bus, truck and plane, must look back on their predecessors of a hundred years ago with considerable envy. This traffic drain was beginning to be felt prior to the Second World War but the huge scale of the conflict and its resultant wear and tear on the railways was all but catastrophic after the war.

In Britain the railways came under governmental control for a second time with freight tonnages soaring and maintenance dropping; the preparations for the D-Day Normandy landings alone required many thousands of special trains. Postwar recovery was slow and it was a decade before money became available for investment in modernization; even then planning was spasmodic, often hindered by politics. One piece of reorganization which will be remembered for a long time was based on the thinking of Dr. Richard Beeching (later Lord Beeching) who had been brought in from industry to chair the

Left: The U.S.A. had denuded itself of steam-hauled passenger trains in the 1950s and sights such as this Chesapeake & Ohio 4-8-4 No. 614 at Prince, West Virginia are now a rarity. Occasionally a few specials can be seen by those in the know, and in 1981 this 22-coach Chessie System Safety Express, which included a dome car, was photographed on its run down the New River Valley from Charleston to Hinton.

British Railways Board and to sort the mess out. The gist of the 'Great and Good' doctor's plan was that the railway must renounce its 19th-century role of common carrier and concentrate on moving traffic in bulk: no more branch lines with sparse services and few passengers, no single wagon loads of coal for suburban or country merchants, no parcels or milk to wayside stations, and no coaches waiting idle in sidings specially for excursion traffic. Everything was to be slimmed down and the unviable axed. But cuts in themselves were not always the answer – for example, branch-line traffic fed mainlines and shared some of the costs, and redundant staff had to be compensated. Nevertheless the Beeching cuts led railway management into new commercial thinking which in its turn has made Britain's railways the least expensive system in Western Europe.

The railways of continental Europe had different problems. Generally they were not just overloaded and worn out, they were devastated. However, because of the political urgency of reconstruction in Western Europe and with the assistance of the Marshall Aid programme from the U.S.A., help was on hand. By the mid-1950s

The introduction of the powerful Deltic locomotives on the East Coast route enabled British Rail's Eastern Region to accelerate its Scottish expresses out of King's Cross station in London. This was the last diesel electric locomotive class to be designed for exclusive express use. Its place has now been taken by the new HST 125 units.

rebuilding had reached such heights that modernization was ahead of that in Britain, who had to struggle on with her own resources – it is always easier to rebuild than to resuscitate.

The U.S.A. also had been hard hit; railroad traffic had increased to almost unprecedented heights during the war, and little money was available for capital replacements. Further problems came once fuel and rubber rationing ceased, allowing cars, buses and trucks to take away traffic, leaving unpleasant cash voids. But there was yet another factor which weighed against American railways, one which the European lines have not had to face – the advent of cheap domestic aviation on the longer hauls. So bad did the situation become that deadly rivals were forced to amalgamate; trains and tracks were abandoned; bankruptcies soon began in earnest. American minds are not attuned to nationalization but it crept in through the back door in another form as even amalgamations failed to stop the rot. (Even the

The Rio Grande Zephyr *as a Union Pacific train runs into Glenwood Springs, Colorado, westbound to Salt Lake City, Utah, behind 3 EMD 29 locomotives in October 1980.*

merging of the rival New York Central and the Pennsylvania Railroad to form the Penn Central came to bankruptcy in the end.) The collapse of mergers and other such disasters led to the formation of the United States Railway Association whose aim was to rationalize a rail network and attempt to make it financially viable. Eventually the Consolidated Rail Corporation, generally known as Conrail, was formed to run a conglomerate of bankrupt systems. Some roads, of course, have survived either in their original form or as amalgamations; for example, the Union Pacific, the Santa Fe and the Rio Grande Western lines are still there, as is the successful Burlington Northern. These few and others like them have stemmed the tide but the long-haul passenger traffic, on the whole, has gone to nationalization under another name. By 1970 the number of long-distance passenger trains had sunk to less than 5 per cent of the 1930s total and extinction was on the cards; they were saved by legislation creating a federally subsidized corporation called AMTRAK which now has the job of running a very much slimmed down intercity passenger network. Canada, too, has a new government passenger agency, VIA Rail, but the freight operation on the Canadian Pacific and the government-owned Canadian National have benefited so much from not having to finance this loss-making traffic that they are now two of the most profitable railways in North America. Conrail has sadly slipped from bad to worse and is at present a political liability; AMTRAK also has its political detractors and some services could be in jeopardy. AMTRAK, however, now has a growing fleet of modern and comfortable rolling stock which, together with new locomotives, gives it a chance. No organization can have had to weather a worse start –

Above: AMTRAK's westbound California Zephyr leaves Glenwood Springs, Colorado, hauled by three F4 OPH diesel electric locomotives in October 1983.

Overleaf: Canada's new look transcontinental. The VIA Rail eastbound Super Continental stands in Jasper station in October 1978 behind three diesel electrics.

67

One of Germany's crack Trans-Europe Expresses, the Rheingold, *is a first class only train. The electrification of the southbound routes out of Cologne enabled a start to be made with faster trains and new standards of comfort.*

battered and worn track, a mixture of equally old and redundant stock rescued from once-proud named trains. It can look to the future even if it is a lean one.

Back in Europe (including the United Kingdom) one of the great success stories has been the intercity passenger train. With shorter distances than those in the U.S.A. and with a far denser population these high-speed trains have managed to compete favourably against road and air. Mention has been made earlier of the European TEE concept; this has now developed into the intercity rail hard-sell made possible by electrification, multiple-unit dieselization and, as exemplified by the French *Trains Grands Vitesse* (TGV) from Paris to Lyons, the construction of a brand new railway.

This bright star in the modern railway firmament has taken the honours from the Japanese Shinkansen high-speed trains. First, the

French have escaped some of the most costly features by using conventional tracks to the outskirts of both Paris and Lyons and second, by *avoiding all towns* en route, it has been possible to build the new railway straight across the great rural areas of France thus obviating the huge cost of construction in urban areas. The TGV is fully compatible with the rest of the French Railways system – it has been built to the same track and loading gauge so that the train sets can continue to run over normal tracks to Marseilles and other cities. All these sets are dual voltage 25kV on the new line, and half power on the 1.5kV routes beyond. Some of these dual voltage sets have also been constructed for use into Switzerland. The newly built route has been constructed to allow for speeds up to 185 mph but at present these are not in force as the SNCF believes that 160 mph gives them the marketing value they require. So automated are these trains that no traditional lineside signalling is installed; locomotive cabs are fitted with a device that allows the driver to set a constant speed up hill and down dale over the steeply undulating route so that he can attend to his primary responsibility of paying attention to the road ahead. There is no question of the great success achieved by the TGV for not only does the Paris-Lyons train out-price anything on the autoroute, but it also produces a far better service than can any airplane city to city. It has been said that the train will probably pluck as many as 75 per cent of the passengers out of the sky on the Lyons route – a noteworthy achievement to say the least.

Overleaf: Switzerland too has some comfortable and fast intercity trains. This set is seen at Aarburg.

Below: France is the bright star in the fast intercity firmament with a direct line of railway from Paris to Lyons and the south. This route for the Trains Grands Vitesse *is completely new, allowing speeds of 160 mph with automated line signalling. So good is the service that road and air cannot compete.*

Below: Today many European motor manufacturers send their bulk supplies by rail. Special double-deck vehicle carriers have been constructed for this traffic. They are used both for car deliveries and for car/sleeper overnight passenger trains. A long train of new cars is seen here running over French Railways' electrified main line.

Nor has Great Britain lagged behind. In spite of the failure of the much-vaunted Advanced Passenger Train with its automatic tilting devices, the other new project, the High Speed Train, has swept the board extremely clean. Entering public service in 1976 on the Western Region mainline, these push-pull units have captured the public imagination with their 125-mph maximum speeds and 90- to 100-mph averages. Today Britain's HST Inter-City image is very high; routes include London to the South West, London to Edinburgh, and an excellent cross-country service from Plymouth to York via Birmingham and Derby. The sharp commercial effect of high-speed and often regular-interval trains has paid off, and aggressive marketing has ensured that the public knows that this is now the 'Age of the Train'. Good timing, a smooth ride, air conditioning and, on the new 'Executive' trains, meals and drinks at passengers' seats have also added to the popularity of these new HSTs. The general design has even been exported under licence to Australia.

North America also has a few intercity expresses. New high-speed trains known as Metroliners were introduced between New York and Washington as early as 1971, becoming part of AMTRAK's remit after the Penn-Central bankruptcy. They are electric multiple units.

Right: Britain's 125 HSTs entered service in 1976: they have been extremely successful, averaging speeds of 90–100 mph. One of the routes using these push-pull units in regular service is that to the southwest from Paddington over Brunel's Great Western tracks, as shown by this up train passing through Sonning cutting.

North America in particular makes good use of the 'piggyback' system when long flat wagons carry huge container trailers between transshipment centres. A westbound TOFAC (trailer on flat car) train of 54 bogies heaves its way up Sherman Hill, Wyoming in October 1983.

Delays, however, have brought troubles to the project, and it has yet to be developed to its full potential. Railroads are not beloved by American politicians.

It took the railways nearly 20 years after the cessation of the Second World War's hostilities to achieve the bulk transportation of freight they were seeking and it was not really until the early 1970s when inflation began in earnest and fuel costs rocketed that the pendulum began to swing back. Two major contributions towards the revival were the introduction of one of today's household words – the container – and an innovation – the car and truck-carrying railcar. Today the major motor manufacturers in many countries send their bulk deliveries by rail. In North America in particular this has been augmented by the 'piggyback' system where long flat wagons transport huge road container vehicles between trans-shipment centres. In fact by the early 1980s this form of traffic was second only in volume to the lucrative carriage of coal. Today the Santa Fe Railroad runs a Los Angeles-Chicago named train, the 'Chief', composed solely of specially constructed articulated vehicles carrying what is now called 'Trailer on Flat Car' (TOFAC) traffic.

Europe also has taken to piggybacks but with more difficulty, due to a restricted loading gauge (impossible in Britain due to even tighter restrictions). Much of this is country-to-country traffic from Europe's

Western industrial areas to countries such as Yugoslavia via Austria, although the French and particularly the Germans have developed internal services with some success.

Bulk freight has come to stay whether it be containers, cars, coal, steel or chemicals. With the formation of the EEC and the general up-surge of international industrial traffic, freight is big business in most countries of the Western world. Unit trains are part of this system as exemplified by British Rail's Merry Go Round (MGR) coal trains where the trains run from pit to power station. At the pits the trains are overhead loaded but on arrival at their destination the track layout is circular and the wagons are unloaded on the move as they are hauled over under-track bunkers at low speed. Coal traffic has always been lucrative and still is, not only in Britain but in Europe and the U.S.A. and Canada (the latter country runs trains of up to 12,000 tons in weight). The unit train has come to stay.

Overleaf: Another type of unit train is Britain's Merry Go Round made up of special coal hoppers which discharge their contents as the train moves slowly over the power station under track bunkers. This heavy train is seen here at Netherton in Cumbria.

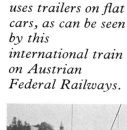

Below: Europe also uses trailers on flat cars, as can be seen by this international train on Austrian Federal Railways.

Left: A huge Canadian National Railway iron ore train crossing a trestle viaduct at South River, Ontario.

Below: Bulk freight in the form of containers is now the mainstay of most of Europe's railways, as can be seen by this West German train heading down the Rhine Valley. Electrification has enabled a faster and intensified service of both fast passenger and freight trains.

Left: Canadian freight is now a very profitable operation as both CP and CN have hived off their non-paying passenger services to the Government sponsored VIA Rail. Two Canadian National Railway diesels head a long freight train down the Fraser River canyon in May 1983.

Concern over supplies of fuel as well as its cost have changed many countries' attitudes to railways in the last decade. Certainly it cannot be disputed that short-distance traffic is the prerogative of the roads but for long-haul freight, rails, particularly on the electrified lines of Europe, provide the cheapest and most efficient operation. Railways now have a more certain future than could have been prophesied in the 1960s; one of the world's busier industries is now railway electrification. The marriage of road and rail, each doing the job to which it is best suited, is now part of most governmental thinking not only from a cost angle but also on an anti-pollution basis.

Trains in the East

With competitive air services bringing down prices from such places as London to Hong Kong, most visitors to the Far East today never even contemplate an overland journey by train. But the train still runs and the ride is far from being uncomfortable. The Trans-Siberian trains begin their journey in Moscow and run through to Vladivostok. However, the presence of the Soviet Pacific Fleet at Vladivostok bars the port to foreigners who have to make do with Khabarovsk. There are 78 stops from Moscow to Khabarovsk and 91 to Vladivostok. The Soviet Union's railway system dominates the country's overland transport scene, moving 75 per cent of the nation's freight and over 50 per cent of its passengers; it is said that the Soviet railways carry over half the world's freight tonnage over some ten per cent of its route mileage. So great is the usage that a new Trans-Siberian route, running from northern Lake Baikal to the Pacific, began construction work in the late 1970s. It will open up an area rich in minerals and valuable metals. Like the huge projects of the 1930s this new route, some 1,995 miles long, has caught popular imagination and the Communist youth organization, Kommsomol, has adopted it. The line runs from Lake Baikal to Amur and Magistral and its route is being blasted through rocky and precipitous terrain as well as virgin forest.

The old Trans-Siberian railway, 5,787 miles in length, is probably one of the most famous lines in the world. Now electrified over its whole length it has reached absolute capacity, binding together the chain of settlements in southern Siberia and carrying, in addition to national supplies, container traffic between Western Europe and Japan. Every four minutes a train passes through the station at Irkutsk, the last major town before Ulan Ude which is the junction for the swing south through Mongolia and into China. Here diesel traction takes over from electric and the heavy flow of traffic declines. The journey from Irkutsk to Ulan Bator, the Mongolian capital, takes around 24 hours and the remaining distance to Peking, a further 24. Today the trains are comfortable and, if Soviet stock is on the through-train, some two-berth soft-class compartments are available. The dining cars are Soviet, Mongolian and Chinese.

In northern China, Japanese influence made its mark in the 1930s; the 'influence' was extended south during the Second World War when the country was overrun. A high proportion of locomotives and rolling stock in operation in the years after the war was of Japanese manufacture or design and, at that time, a considerable number of

The route of the Trans-Siberian Railway.

The Forbidden City. Vladivostock station, the eastern terminus of the Trans-Siberian Railway. Foreigners are not allowed to make the journey beyond Khabarovsk and boat trains with connections to Japan are routed to the port of Nakhodka.

The comfortable interior of a typical Russian dining car as found on the Trans-Siberian trains.

American locomotives were also sent to China to help rehabilitate the railways. Times were hard. Before 1935 and the Japanese occupation, the country had some 12,000 miles of railway; by 1949 less than half was operational, having been destroyed by the years of internal struggle and disorder.

The People's Republic of China was proclaimed in 1949 and the new government found itself faced with the huge task of repair and reconstruction. The scale of the task was immense. For example, the Five Year Plan beginning in 1958 envisaged the construction of 55 new lines and the reconstruction or double tracking of 29 others. By 1964 the length of operating railways was estimated to be over 20,000

*Left: Peking
station, People's
Republic of China.
Completed in the
late 1950s it
provides more than
adequate facilities
for all passengers.
A Peking-built
2500 HP diesel
hydraulic
locomotive stands
in the terminus
after arriving with
a train from the
Mongolian border
– a through service
from Moscow.*

miles. Prior to 1949 seven large provinces had no railways; today none is without, and a line is even being constructed deep into Tibet. In 1964 there was virtually no signalling; today some of the most modern and sophisticated systems in the world are in use. With a total length of railway line now close to 30,000 miles and still expanding, the main routes form a grid pattern. North-South routes run from Beijing to Shanghai and to Guangzhou and from Baoji to Kumming, the last being recently built through almost impossible mountain terrain in the far southwest. East-West trunk routes run from Shanghai to Kumming and from Lian Yun Kang on the east coast to Wulumuchi in Sinkiang. Through passenger trains run from Beijing to Moscow (U.S.S.R.), Pyonyang (North Korea), Ulan Bator (Mongolia), and (with a change to metre gauge) to Hanoi (Vietnam). In 1980 the number of passengers carried reached over one hundred million.

Electrification is beginning in China but much more use is made of diesel locomotives, particularly diesel hydraulics, most of which are built in China's own workshops. Some are based on German Henschel designs with Maybach-inspired engines while others bear the imprint

*Overleaf:
Sightseeing No. 1.
A double-headed
train of both soft
and hard seats seen
at Quinglingqiao in
1980. There are
three Great Wall
trains out of
Peking daily, two
hauled by QJ class
2-10-2 steam
locomotives.*

*Below: The
reserved seat
booking
department Peking
station.*

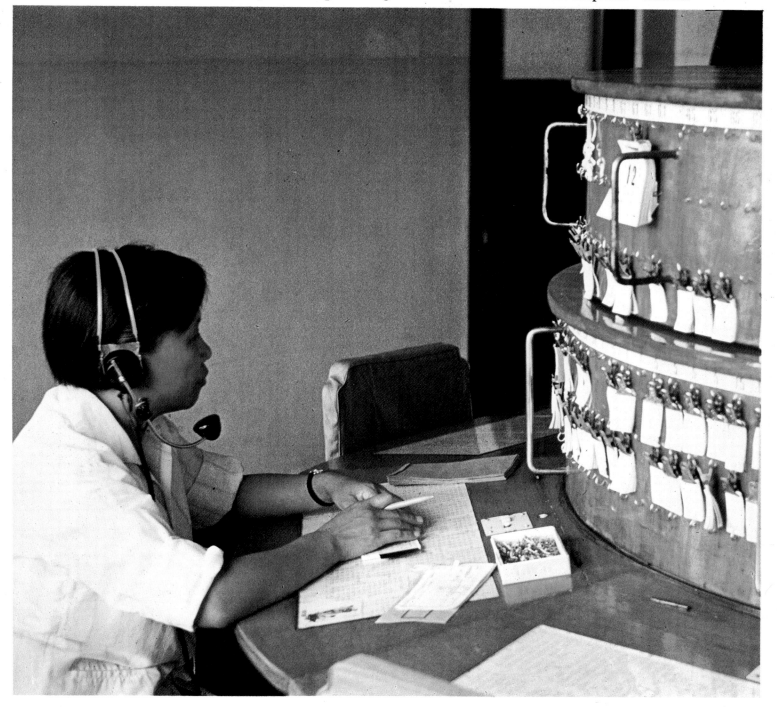

Above: Start the day right. Hard class passengers making use of station facilities in the early morning on a train from Peking to Shanghai.

of American, French, Romanian and Soviet influence. To ensure steady and reliable progress the Chinese have secured advice from the world's most knowledgable sources.

Steam is very much alive in China with the RM (People's) and SL (Victory) classes of 4-6-2s hard at work on the secondary expresses over large areas of the country. Other modern classes include the huge QJ (Advance Forward) 2-10-2s and the JS (Construction) class 2-8-2s as well as the older and very numerous JF varieties of 2-8-2. In China steam engines are well cared for and clean.

Freight traffic over China's main trunk routes is heavy and intense with loads averaging 3,000 tons, well within the capacity of the new diesels and the QJ 2-10-0s. Long-distance passenger trains are also heavy, running normally to 12 or 14 standard units of coaches, mostly hard class, with what are known as semi-cushioned berths as well as a dining car, luggage vans, a coach for the attendants and two or three soft-class sleepers with four berths to a compartment. Generally these trains are diesel-hauled. The train from Beijing for Guangzhou makes the journey in 33 hours, covering 1,500 or so miles and making 11 stops, most of which are only of three minutes' duration.

Right: A 3,000-ton freight train headed by QJ (Forward) class 2-10-2 No. 823 crosses the huge Yangtze River bridge at Wuhan in May 1983. The decorations and slogans are encouraged by the authorities; loco crews are able to gain commendation for care of their machine and fuel economy.

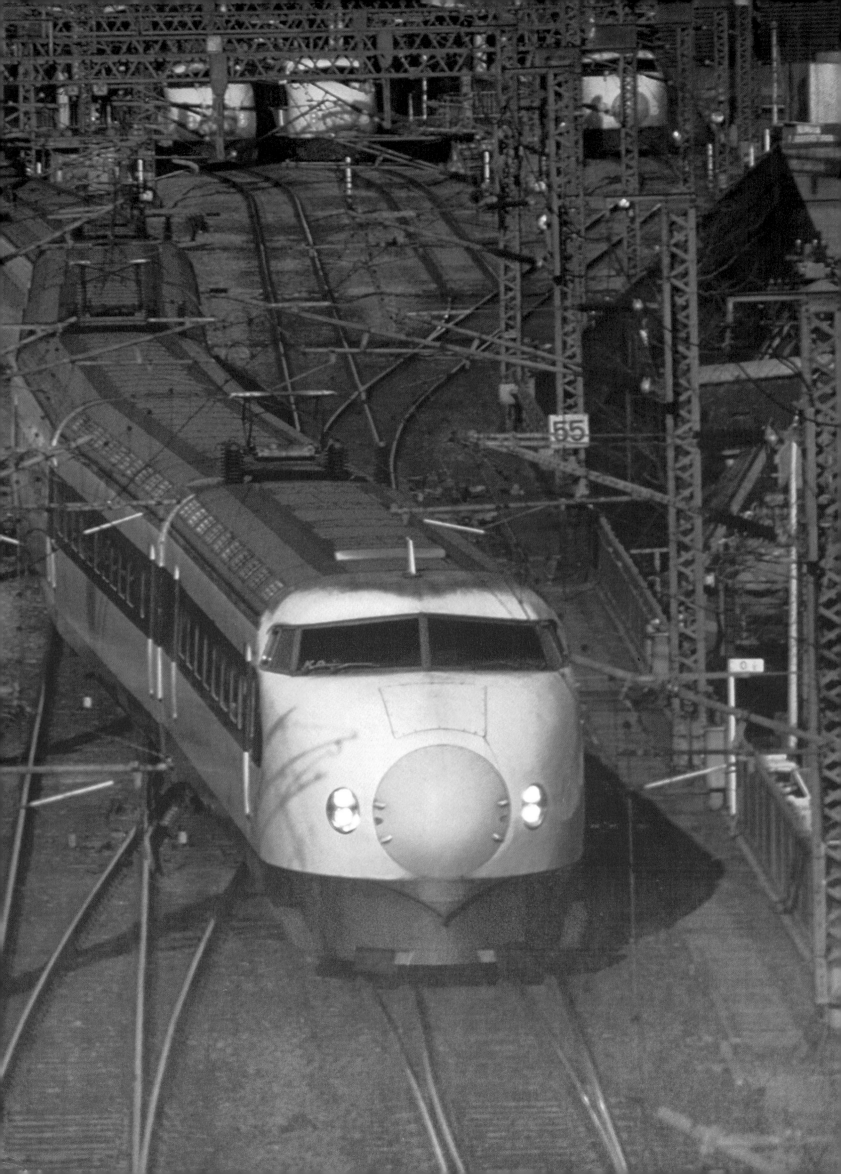

Further east, Japan has made different but equally tremendous strides where passenger traffic outstrips freight by as much as five to one – a situation quite contrary to accepted practice elsewhere. Japan's railways were built to the narrow gauge of 3 ft 6 in and, in consequence, both speed and capacity were somewhat restricted. This applied especially in the most populous area, known as the Tokaido, which stretches for 320 miles along the shore of the main island of Honshu from Tokyo to Osaka. Some 40 per cent of Japan's population and over 70 per cent of its industry is concentrated in this area. Somewhat naturally Japan's first mainline railway was built here and, after the Second World War, traffic began to increase at a tremendous rate. So much did the traffic increase that by the 1970s it became obvious that the railway would be unable to cope. Japanese minds bent to the problem and came up with the idea of an entirely new railway on the wider gauge of 4 ft 8½ in. The idea was revolutionary not only

Left: Close-up view of a Bullet Train leaving the yards in Tokyo. This completely new railway has been built to the 4 ft 8½ in gauge and is solely passenger carrying.

Left: One of Japan's New Tokaido Line trains on the Tokyo to Osaka route with Mt. Fuji in the background.

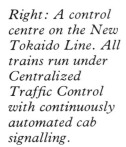

Right: A control centre on the New Tokaido Line. All trains run under Centralized Traffic Control with continuously automated cab signalling.

Below: Malaysian Railways have kept two of their one-time express Pacific locomotives to haul tourist trains from Kuala Lumpur to Batu Caves. Sadly, these are now in unlined black when once they were the pride of the line in Great Western green.

in its concept of cutting a swathe through town and country but also because with the new gauge the line would be solely passenger carrying. The new railway was 25 miles shorter than the old and among the remarkable engineering works completed must be included two long tunnels, each nearly five miles long, and great viaducts whose spans are carried on pneumatic caissons which had to be sunk to depths of over 50 ft (15 m) to find firm foundations.

The New Tokaido Line has ten intermediate stations between Tokyo and Osaka (that is, in the 320 miles). It is very much a high-speed railway with trains travelling at up to 130 mph under Centralized Traffic Control with no exterior signals, and movement completely automated with continuous cab signalling. From an initial 60,000 passengers daily over the line at the time of opening, the number had grown to 113,000 in two years, 151,000 three years later, and by 1970 near 350,000. It is a one-class-only railway with 12-coach trains seating over one thousand passengers. The line is called the Shinkansen or 'new railway' and the trains, 'Bullet Trains'.

In the 1970s the line was projected beyond Osaka to Hakata, crossing from Honshu to Kyushu Island via a new 11½-mile tunnel which is the second longest in the world (after the Swiss Simplon). Trains on this extension are less speedy because of geological conditions. New sections, this time progressing in a northerly direction from Tokyo to Morioka and Niigata, are under construction. These new lines have been designed to allow for speeds up to 160 mph but in view of the fact that the original route has had to relaid and rewired after only ten years of intensive use, the Japanese have baulked at a commitment to operate a daily system at this higher speed although the 130 mph is to continue in spite of the high cost and a somewhat noisy environmental image. Although the Shinkansen is not the world's fastest railway (this accolade belongs to the French Paris-Lyons route), it is a very great achievement and its 'Bullet Trains' have undoubtedly produced worldwide business for their countrymen.

Back on the mainland and further south, the railway system of Malaysia has brought prosperity to the jungle, for here the railway pioneered the jungle route long before roads were made: prior to the railway's arrival the Malays found waterways more than adequate for their transportation. Today the metre-gauge system operates over a track exceeding 1,000 miles and runs modern air-conditioned trains. There is still a miniscule amount of steam, kept mostly for tourist use over the branch from Kuala Lumpur to Batu Caves. The engines are

The modern station at Hat Yai junction with a southbound train for the Malaysian border behind a Thai Railways diesel electric locomotive. Steam, which was well in evidence in Thailand a decade ago, is now virtually extinct.

A WG class 2-8-2 stands in the modern station in Delhi. India, though rapidly electrifying its main lines, still uses vast numbers of steam locomotives including many Baldwins ordered just prior to Independence.

cared for as well as possible under today's conditions but in their dull black livery they cannot uphold the splendour of the old days when they appeared in the colours of the old Great Western Railway – dark green with polished brasswork and copper capped chimneys – an expatriate's dream of Swindon past.

North of Malaysia, Thailand's railways complete the link from Singapore to Bangkok and the north Indo-Chinese border. Diesels came early to Thailand; some were used even prior to the Second World War on the southern mainline where the service from the capital to Penang took 26 hours, with a full dining- and sleeping-car service. Times have changed in the Far East but train travel is still a fascinating mixture of old and new – and sometimes an adventure.

Further west is the huge railway system which belongs to India. It has a track mileage approaching 40,000 and employs about 5 per cent of the population. What is more, there are three distinct gauge classifications: standard 5 ft 6 in; sub-standard metre; and narrow which is normally 2 ft 6 in.

India, Pakistan and Bangladesh are all Meccas to the steam-locomotive enthusiast and India's Chittaranjan works (set up in 1950) has only recently ceased steam construction; now it builds diesels and electrics but has a heavy steam overhaul and repair programme. Electrification is pressing ahead and about 14 per cent of the broad-gauge track comes under wires today. India's railways are colourful and provide a wonderful opportunity to see mixtures of old and new, and of East and a small modicum of West. Modern motive power may head the train and some coaches may be air-conditioned but old practices die hard; one still wakes up on the 'Mail' from the Himalayas to Delhi and orders breakfast at the station from the compartment window, has it delivered piping hot on a tray at the next station, and has the empty plates collected at the next. To travel on the narrow gauge is to go back three generations.

Trains in Africa and Australasia

Cecil Rhodes's great dream of a Cape-to-Cairo railway certainly captured the imagination but although tracks forged their way northwards to the borders of the then-Belgian Congo, they never progressed further.

British enterprise gave Africa its first railway – that from Cairo to Alexandria – as early as 1854. Laid to the standard gauge of 4 ft 8½ in it followed general European practice – it was built and operated on lines similar to the railways at home. By the time Rhodes was active in the south, railways had already been thriving in northern Africa. The railway systems of the French colonies of Algeria and Tunisia followed those of France while the Spanish gained a small toe-hold in Morocco. The Italians came later and their tracks were mainly narrow gauge in Ethiopia, Eritrea, Somaliland and Libya: in the former countries these systems were driven through mountains, requiring the construction of magnificent high viaducts and long tunnels. The German development in East Africa came to an end in 1918; the Belgians were successful in tapping the vital mineral resources of the Congo. East Africa was developed by the British and after the First World War the metre-gauge Kenya & Uganda Railway (later East African

Angola once provided a vital economic link between landlocked Northern Rhodesia (now Zambia) and the Atlantic coast via the Benguela Railway which ran from the border of Zaire and the South Atlantic port of Lobito. Even in the early 1970s this opulent dining car was in regular use on the overnight train to Nova Lisboa.

Railways when combined with Tanzania) was a really superb system; now it is uneconomically fragmented by nationalism. The seemingly odd gauge was used simply because at the time of construction, the British had some surplus metre-gauge equipment in India.

The same national fragmentation now applies to the railways in South Africa. Once the Cape Gauge connected a vast area of Africa like a spider's web. The British, Belgian and Portuguese tracks even provided a service (via the British-owned Benguela Railway) from the west coast port of Lobito in Angola to Cape Town, or across to the Indian ocean at Beira; indeed 60 per cent of Africa's track mileage is in the south.

Left: East African Railways once had a really fine metre gauge system linking Uganda and Kenya to the Indian Ocean at Mombasa; today it is fragmented by tribal independence. The EAR ran oil-burning steam locomotives until well into the 1970s and most locomotives were fitted with the fuel-saving, spark-arresting Giesl ejector. Class 29 2-8-2 No. 2905 is so fitted as it leaves Nairobi with a Nakuru-bound freight in December 1975.

Left: With the breakup of East African Railways, Nairobi became the headquarters of the new Kenya Railways, and liveries changed from red to blue, as seen by these Henschel 660-hp diesels waiting to enter the yards in May 1978.

Overleaf: South African Railways have always kept their locomotives in beautiful condition, often being named and decorated by their crews. A non-condensing 4-8-4 heads towards Kimberley with a train of vans in 1977. These class 25 NCs are still in mainline use, Kimberley shed being one of their main stabling points.

Above: A Rhodesia Railways train behind Garratt No. 422 as it makes its way up the gradient from Victoria Falls bridge where it has picked up a train of copper bars from Zambia in 1973. The train will have been pushed over the centre line of the bridge for the RR locomotive to collect.

West Africa, a patchwork of jungle, mountains and desert, had railways constructed by the Germans, French and British with little interconnection between them.

The original concept of the African railways was two-fold: to provide good military communications (especially on the Mediterranean coast) and to establish the most economical way of conveying raw materials extracted from the interior to the coast. No one could possibly have thought that any one line in, say, British Southern Africa could have ever wished to be entirely interdependent on its next door neighbour. So the railway problems of the African Third World are considerable – where inter-communication is concerned nationalism has its drawbacks.

An example of such a problem was that of land-locked Zambia which, prior to Zimbabwe becoming a nation, had no access to the port of Beira on the Indian Ocean in adjacent Mozambique. This problem was eventually overcome in 1967 when the Chinese financed and built what is now known as the Tan-Zam Railway linking

Left: The world's most luxurious train – the South African Railways' Blue Train on its way from Cape Town to Johannesburg behind two electric locomotives. Such is the comfort that three-roomed suites as well as sumptuous dining and bar services are provided for those willing to pay.

Zambian Railways with the Tanzanian coast. Sadly, after only a few years of untrained African operation, the Chinese have had to return to keep the wheels turning.

With the problems arising from the Tan-Zam line, there were commercial difficulties in moving copper exports out of Zambia: the line to the west coast via Angola was closed because of internal strife, causing acute embarrassment. The Benguela Railway in the early 1970s and prior to Angolan independence, was so busy that new locomotives in the form of diesels had been ordered to help to move the traffic where freight trains were running block and block over the long single line westwards. There was only one solution – to take the traffic south over the tracks of the then-Rhodesian Railways and out through South Africa, however unpalatable that might be.

Even though a state of, to say the least, noncommunication, existed between Lusaka and Salisbury, these trains still ran. The traffic crossed the border over Cecil Rhodes's Victoria Falls bridge with at least one long train a day moving in each direction – grain in, Zambian copper out. The procedure was simple: on arrival at Victoria Falls the

The Garden Route, a two-night, one-day journey from Cape Town to Port Elizabeth, is one of Africa's most scenic routes. For many years the tracks from Cape Town to Worcester have been electrified and now the diesels have taken over the remainder. In the days of steam this was partly a

Garratt operation with the locomotives running bunker first because of the tunnels. These two photographs show a train on the climb up from George to the summit. Right: In 1971 looking from the rear of the train. Below: In 1975 looking across the valley at what seems to be a model railway.

huge Rhodesian steam Garratt locomotive would run round its train and push it down to the bridge so that most of the wagons ran over the centre border; the train was collected later by a Zambian engine. A similar process would work in reverse, the Zambians pushing their trainload of copper over on to the Rhodesian side. The stationmasters at Victoria Falls and Livingstone had a special telephone line for this arrangement.

No mention of Southern Africa can be complete without a reference to South African Railway's most famous and luxurious train running from Cape Town to Johannesburg and Pretoria - the 'Blue Train'. The service itself is nothing new for as far back as the Edwardian era a luxury train connected the two cities, and even in the 1930s the 'Union Limited', as it was called, carried an observation lounge, a bar and sleepers complete with showers. Today's train, new in 1972, is one of absolute luxury. It is 16 coaches long and includes one car which only carries six passengers, has twin beds, a separate lounge and a full-sized bathroom. Such a train is far from economic but such is its national prestige that the service is unlikely to be withdrawn – tourist trade counts for much today.

During the last decade times have changed for Africa's railways, mostly for the worse. Gone is the vast traffic over the Benguela Railway in Angola; gone are the luxurious East African Railway trains linking Kampala, Nairobi and Mombasa, hauled by spotless red Garratt locomotives; and gone for the enthusiast are the great steam-hauled trains over the Garden Route from Cape Town to Port Elizabeth in South Africa – the diesels have taken over. But there are considerable plusses. It is now possible, once again, to take a passenger train over the Victoria Falls bridge and catch the spray from the falls as you go; for the rail fan Zimbabwe is full of interest with the economic development of its railway system growing apace: the resuscitation of dozens of Garratts for further use, introduction of new diesel power, and electrification out of Harare (Salisbury). In northern Africa there has also been progress. The Egyptian State Railways, for example, have introduced high-class sleeping- and dining-car services from Cairo down to the Valley of the Kings at Luxor and beyond to Aswan.

Right: An interstate freight train in the Avon Valley, Western Australia. Note the mixed make-up of this train, piggyback road vehicles, containers and box cars, also the dual gauge track – Western Australia uses 3 ft 6 in gauge whilst the interstate line is 4 ft 8½ in.

Right: Western Australia's narrow gauge of 3 ft 6 in does not inhibit the haulage of heavy unit traffic, as can be seen by these two DB diesel electric locomotives at the head of a bauxite train. The railway uses the name Westrail.

Right: Australia's great Intercontinental train – the Indian Pacific. Until 1969 it was impossible to make a railway journey from New South Wales to Western Australia without a change of gauge. Now this air-conditioned train with de luxe first class accommodation makes the journey over 4 ft 8½ in gauge tracks all the way.

Below: One of the last of the AD60 class of 4-8-4 + 4-8-4 Beyer Garratts still in regular service takes a special north of Newcastle NSW in August 1972. The last of the class in service was No. 6042 – withdrawn in March 1973, the year of final steam working on all Government systems.

106

A Co-Co electric No. 4638 pilots 4-8-4 + 4-8-4 Garratt No. 6018 on a Sydney bound freight train up the 1 in 35 Cowan bank between Hawksbury River and Cowan, thirty four miles north of the state capital on 9th January 1960. This was only two weeks prior to full electric working taking over from steam.

Australia today sees a great future for its railways and considerable steps have been taken to overcome the old multi-gauge problems. A new image has been created under the name Railways of Australia, an organization sponsored by all State systems. It involves joint owner-ship of rolling stock for through services (including the Sydney-Perth 'Indian Pacific Express') and of mechanical bogie changing equipment at gauge-change points (Melbourne, Peterborough and Port Pirie). There is also a new standard gauge (4 ft 8½ in) line open to link Adelaide with Broken Hill. West to east through-working has only been in operation for half a generation. In 1968 the Western Australian Government Railway completed its standard-gauge line linking Kwinana, Fremantle and Perth, with the Trans-Australian western terminus at Kalgoorlie while the last section, the South Australian Government's line from Port Pirie to the New South Wales network at Broken Hill, opened in January 1970. This gives a total east-west distance of 2,461 miles including nearly 300 miles across the Nullabor plain where the track is absolutely straight. Originally the journey meant travelling over three different gauges: 3 ft 6 in (Western Australia), 5 ft 3 in (South Australia) and 4 ft 8½ in (New South Wales). Today, passengers travel on one of the world's luxury trains, the 'Indian Pacific'. First-class travel includes a cocktail-lounge bar with writing tables and, maintaining the old trans-Australian tradition, a piano.

Although Australia has joined other countries in denying its railways investment capital in the mid- and late 20th-century years and even though air competition is extreme on long-haul routes, there are a number of excellent intercity trains, some of considerable comfort. Air-conditioned sleepers are the norm as well as twinette berths with toilets. Often a club car is carried as well as a diner and it is a strong

Tasmania uses the 3 ft 6 in gauge and steam is now only a memory. However, this MA class 4-6-2, No. 4, was photographed at Launceston as late

as 1970. Ten of these engines were built by Robert Stephenson & Co. in 1952 based on the Indian Railways' metre gauge Xb class.

European who can stand up to a full Australian railway breakfast. Freight, too, is heavy with block and unit trains very much to the fore, some of immense tonnages. In fact, some of the heaviest trains in the world are Australian freights carrying iron-ore deposits in Western Australia to coastal ports.

New Zealand's 3 ft 6 in gauge railways have also undergone modernization. Standards have been improved in intercity North Island expresses (not before time) and here also bulk freight transportation has brought new life.

Railways of Character

Moat Lane Junction on the one-time Cambrian Railway. The branch train behind a modern post-Second World War 2-6-0 running tender first is bound for Three Cocks Junction where it meets yet another branch from Hereford to Brecon. Modern motive power did not save this Mid-Wales line.

In the West today the railway has only three real functions: the carriage of heavy long-haul containerized freight; the movement of passengers on fast intercity trains; and the suburban, interurban or urban lines. All incorporate modern thinking with modern technology; each because of economic necessity, is as near automation as it is sensibly possible to devise.

Although the customers, the passengers and, one hopes, the operators and the environment gain immensely from this brave new railway world, there is a lack-lustre present today which the trains of yesteryear overcame. Missing today is the human touch, the throb and thrust of steam power, the little country lines which are few and far between. Once, when the railway had a monopoly, it was an inevitable part of everyone's life – the only way to travel! Its variety was almost infinite; style, liveries, architecture, and comfort varied from line to line, district to district and country to country. Competition between lines only added to one's pleasure. In those days, which were not *always* good, rail travel was a form of adventure and never more so than when taking a train which left the mainline behind at some country junction. These little railways were the veins which fed the arteries; sometimes they were just branch lines, sometimes they were built to the narrow gauge and sometimes they did not even carry passengers –

Narrow gauge no more. Although the U.S.A. still has two scenic and popular steam worked narrow gauge lines working as tourist railways in the summer (at Durango and Alamosa in Colorado), these are only sections of a once great system. This was the narrow gauge empire of the Denver & Rio Grande Western Railroad which, along with its connecting but even more spectacular sister, the Rio Grande Southern, are part of Colorado folklore. The Rio Grande Southern was the first to go – as early as 1951.

just freight from the local quarry or mine. Generally speaking these links between village and market town, market town and port, or mine and rail head are now gone, replaced by paved roads with their attendant cars, buses and trucks. There are no narrow-gauge railways as common carriers left now in the United Kingdom, few in Europe and few if any in the U.S.A. although there are some short lines still operating. Most of those still working in the West are tourist oriented; those in Eastern Europe, Africa and the Far East still run because economic and political conditions deny private motorized transport to the common man.

For those with eyes to see, some of these rail lines of local interest are still there, some flourishing (but not many), some (indeed most) state supported, and some tottering towards the last buffer stop. To see them, one needs time, patience, and a good constitution.

Apart from a few short lines in the U.S.A. and Canada, the North American continent and the U.K. have no such individualistic railways left, bar those given over to tourism; the same can be said for most of Western Europe though here there are a few pockets of considerable fascination and interest. For example, there are no less than three narrow-gauge systems operating in tourist-stricken Majorca, and visits to both Spain and Portugal are far from unrewarding. Eastern Europe, also, is a different story.

In the socialist-oriented states there is still much to savour. The German Democratic Republic has, for example, a network of narrow-gauge lines, all steam-worked, which serve areas from the Hartz mountains to the Polish and Czech borders. Here one can find old Saxon-Meyer tanks, Mallets and modern ten-coupled oil-burning locomotives hauling freight tankers on modern transporter wagons. In Poland, steam is also to the fore on narrow-gauge lines. Further south,

Overleaf: Even tourist-stricken Majorca has its fascinating little railways, albeit a mere shadow of their former selves. Once the Majorca Railway had steam, with a main line running out of Palma and a harbour branch running through a tunnel under the huge cathedral. Now it is truncated, but railcars still run. It is siesta time at Palma station in November 1982.

111

Above: One of East Germany's most interesting lines is the 76 cm gauge railway running from Wolkenstein to Johstadt, which not only uses transporter wagons to carry standard gauge interchange freight but also unique 0-4-0 + 0-4-0 Saxon Meyer articulated locomotives.

Bulgaria and Yugoslavia have narrow-gauge sections of their state railways which take the traveller far away from the beaten track. Yugoslavia had, until recently, a huge network of 76-cm tracks ranging from Belgrade southwards to the Adriatic coast via Sarajevo, much of it passing through Second World War partisan country in the Bosnian mountains.

For those with strong hearts, Syria has a narrow-gauge system and the Royal Hashemite Railway in Jordan joins it for a trip to Amman. Turkey, much more welcoming, has standard-gauge tracks which take one into its more primitive parts with scenery that can only be described as magnificent. Accommodation here, however, is sometimes only for the hardy.

India, Pakistan and Sri Lanka abound with lines of character – who could expect much else in the East where each is his own man? Even on the Indian mainline it is not unknown for the train on a single track to reverse a short distance because the driver has dropped the tablet, or someone has pulled the communication cord on the outskirts of a city and jumped off to avoid a long walk home. In Pakistan, on the Khyber line out of Peshawar, one must ride in the engine cab for

Left: Turkey still uses steam on the Asian side of the Bosphorus including the line out of Izmir to Afyon – a very hilly route, usually needing double heading in spite of the use of a German 'Kreigslok' 2-10-0 locomotive. Most steam is even further to the East.

safety if he (or she) is European. Sri Lanka still runs Hunslet 4–6–4 tanks on its 2 ft 6 in gauge tracks out of Colombo and beyond Kandy there are working elephants in the forest.

Africa is so full of individualistic railways that it would take a whole book to describe them; sadly many are in countries where nationalism forbids close interest or insurrection has caused services to be abandoned. Once, in Angola and Mozambique, one could see wood-burning Garratts on the night mail from the coast up to Nova Lisboa, and narrow-gauge Baldwins and Alcos on the banks of the Limpopo River. South Africa still provides a haven of interest for the rail fan. Even though the tracks over the Garden Route are dieselized today, the narrow-gauge lines in Cape Province and Natal still use some steam.

The ex-Dutch Spice Islands, now Indonesia, once had some of the finest metre-gauge railways in the world with fast expresses between the principal towns. Now with independence, times have changed. After a long period of deterioration the main routes of the railway system carry fast diesel trains between the major cities, but branch and secondary lines, generally in a run-down state, often use ageing steam power including Mallets and elderly 4-4-0s. Until very recently some 0-4-0s were at work on the north coast of Java. Sumatra has one of the few non-tourist steam-operated rack railways in the world

Not always the easiest country to visit, Syria does not put up the bars to those with a railway interest. Main line trains into Jordan are dieselized but some 2-8-2s still work out of Damascus. No. 260 leaves, tender first, with a train for the works.

where Swiss-, German- or Japanese-built 0-10-0 tanks blast their way through the jungle, though today the trains are freight only. Even this scene is changing with the introduction of new diesel rack locomotives. However, because of the repair facilities available, steam is likely to be in reserve for a long time yet.

South America still remains one of the finest areas for lines full of individualism. The difficulty for the enthusiast here, however, is that these railways are few and spread themselves over a vast continent and many different countries – some in the Andes, some in the heat of Paraguay and others in the pampas of the Argentine. In the northwest of the continent there are two state-owned systems which are nominally dieselized but which, when costly repairs and spares have to be bought or found, bring out steam. These are located in Ecuador and on the narrow-gauge sections of the Peruvian railway. The situation will not last much longer, for the Ecuador line is in danger of closure and in Peru diesels have all but taken over.

The Guayaquil & Quito is the principal line of the Ecuadorian State Railways and although not matching the over 15,000 ft (4,572 m) summit of the old 'Central' of Peru it climbs to over 10,000 ft (3,050 m) in 50 miles, once the 54 miles of flat river-delta lands have been left behind at Bucay. Passenger service, or rather *the* passenger service, is a daily railcar in each direction, but if one has the time the 'real' way to ride is on the tender of the Baldwin 2-8-0 hauling the 'Mixto', which takes most of the day to cover the mountain section to

India abounds with lines of character in all its variety of gauges. Of these the narrow gauge lines have to be seen to be believed, for time has almost stood still. In 1978 a McLeod's Bankura to Damodar River Railway 2 ft 6 in gauge 0-6-4 tank pauses for photography as water buffaloes look on.

117

Right: Sri Lanka still uses its narrow gauge railway out of Colombo though this has now been severely cut back and dieselized. Three of its Hunslet built 4-6-4 tanks are still in working order, and one of these can be seen at work daily in and out of the Fort Station – usually over the shorter distances.

Riobamba, including the hair-raising ascent of the Devil's Nose by means of reverses. Travel by train in Ecuador is cheap, very cheap, and on the 'Mixto' the cost is minimal compared with the road bus (it needs to be as it takes six times as long). Time has little meaning to the South American Indian who makes up the passenger complement – some ride in the coach, some on the roof and some on the loco's tender. Here the railway is much more than just a means of transport – it is part of the way of life for the mountain people. Station stops provide hot water from the engine injectors for washing clothes, opportunities for sending parcels to friends or relatives and time to make minor repairs to the locomotive. The 'Mixto' is also a trading post, especially on the journey from the coast. Newspaper sellers ride on the tender to be first out with the papers from Guayaquil and passengers bring fruit such as bananas and pineapples from the tropical lowlands as well as fish, to be bartered for and haggled over en route or at their destination.

Java, the principal Indonesian island, is not tourist orientated. It does, however, appeal greatly to the enthusiast as it is the last place in the world to use Mallet type locomotives; these work between Cibatu, Garut and Tjakajang.

Above: Indonesia's other large island, Sumatra, has another piece of wondrous railway – a steam-operated rack line centred on Padang Panjang. Although new diesels have been imported with overseas aid, steam is still at large. In this photograph one of the 1960s' built Japanese 0-10-0 rack engines pushes its way up through the jungle to Padang Panjang in 1979.

Left: Ferrocarriles Ecuatorianos – the Guayaquil & Quito. Indian passengers wait patiently for the Mixto in November 1981.

Above: Peru is famous for its railways of the Andes. Huancayo is also the terminus of a metre gauge section to Huancuvilica, the whole of this running at a height of 10–11,000 ft (3,050 m). Until 1983 steam, in the form of Henschel 2-8-2s, worked the local 'Indian' trains. One of these is seen here at Huancayo in 1976.

In Peru there are two spectacular mainlines: the route of the old 'Central' from Lima to Huancayo high in the Andes via a summit reached by zigzags; and the route of the 'Southern' of Peru from Cuzco to Mollendo and Puno. The branch from Juliaca to Puno ends at the northwestern tip of the highest navigable lake in the world – Lake Titicaca – and from here, once a week, a steamer makes the connection and travels overnight to Bolivia. The oldest and most interesting of five such ships is the S.S. *Inca* which was built at Hull in England. It was sailed across the Atlantic, around Cape Horn and up the Pacific Coast to Mollendo. It was then dismantled and shipped by rail to Puno where it was put together again and finally launched on the lake. Sadly the Peruvians are ashamed of its age and have obliterated the date on its polished brass maker's plate.

The Andean terminus at Huancayo meets a narrow-gauge section (metre), now almost completely dieselized, which continues over the mountains to remote Huancavilica while that at Cuzco, capital of the Incas, connects with the old Santa Anna railway (also metre gauge) which runs to Puente Ruinas, the station for the incredible Machu Picchu, a virtually intact Inca city set high in a mountain redoubt.

Overleaf: Mountain railroading. A Baldwin 2-8-0 No. 53 of the Guayaquil and Quito Railway waits at Sibambe in the Andes of Ecuador in November 1981. The engine is an oil burner whilst behind the tender is the long arm of the water crane. The train is waiting to pass the daily Mixto from Riobamba.

A fleet of well maintained Baldwin 2-8-0s and 4-6-0s work the narrow gauge line of the São João del Rei in the Belo Horizonte region.

This railway also reaches its height out of Cuzco by means of a series of reverse zigzags. Both narrow-gauge railways have some steam power but this is now only used in an emergency or for transfer services between standard- and narrow-gauge stations.

Not that the railways mentioned are the only lines to cross the Andes – others equally spectacular connect Bolivia with Chile and Chile with the Argentine. But all the lines on the South American continent are full of interest, from vast sugar railways in Brazil which use old American steam power (Brazil also has the unique 75-cm

gauge São Jāo del Rei with a fleet of colourful Baldwins) to the German-built narrow-gauge steam locos which run through bleak Welsh Patagonia towards the Chilean border. Last, but certainly far from least, and off the tourist track, are the railway systems of Uruguay and Paraguay. Both employ British-built steam engines which emerge from colonial-style termini. The locos of Paraguay trundle over grass-grown tracks heading the 'International Train' to Buenos Aires. If one has the time, the constitution and the will, all this can be enjoyed for a relative pittance.

In many of the Third World countries these railways of character are likely to be active for years to come, though steam is very much on the wane; indeed it is far beyond the eleventh hour. No more are being built except in China. The coming of the diesel is an integral part of Western aid and this, coupled with the lack of availability of steam spares, must mean that before too long the internal combustion engine will totally obliterate the one machine which has never been capable of conversion to warlike use.

But whatever the motive power, these survivors are there for the very reason that men pioneered the lines of a hundred and fifty years ago – to serve the local people. Because of this they are truly lines of character and should be visited on every excuse – not only for one's enjoyment but also to find out how the world goes round beyond the boundaries of comfortable materialism.

The principal South American railway stations, especially those in the capital cities, are reminders of a proud past, as can be seen here in this night shot of Uruguay's monumental General Artigas station in Montevideo.